Surprise!
It's
Gluten-Free!

Surprise!

It's Gluten-Free!

Entrées, breads & desserts so delicious you won't know what's missing

Jennifer Fisher

ALPHA

Publisher Mike Sanders
Editor Alexandra Andrzejewski
Designer and Art Director Rebecca Batchelor
Photographer Kelley Schuyler
Food Stylist Lovoni Walker
Chef Ashley Brooks
Recipe Tester Trish Sebben Malone
Proofreaders Polly Zetterberg, Lisa Himes
Indexer Brad Herriman

First American Edition, 2021
Published in the United States by DK Publishing
6081 E. 82nd Street, Indianapolis, IN 46250

Library of Congress Catalog Number: 2020941353
ISBN: 978-1-6156-4973-0

DK books are available at special discounts when purchased
in bulk for sales promotions, premiums, fund-raising,
or educational use. For details, contact:
SpecialSales@dk.com

Printed and bound in China

Photographs on pages 9 and 192 © Jeff Stay

All other images © Dorling Kindersley Limited

For the curious

www.dk.com

To my boys,
my biggest fans
and inspirations

Contents

Introduction 8

Gluten-Free Basics &
Essential Flour Blends 12

Wheat-Free Mornings 26

Fish & Poultry Mains 42

Pork & Beef Mains 62

Flour-Free Sides & Soups 84

Perfect Pizzas & Breads 102

Sweet Loaves, Muffins &
Scones 118

Pies & Fruity Desserts 136

Cakes & Cupcakes 150

Brownies & Cookies 168

Index 188

Acknowledgments 192

Introduction

It All Revolves Around Food

Food is so much more than fuel—it's intertwined with family, friendships, holidays, and memories. As an adult, when I eat the same foods my parents fed me as a child—stir-fry, white chicken enchiladas, sloppy Joes, chicken divan, and enchilada pie—it takes my memory decades back.

When I think of gathering with family and friends for the holidays, I think of the Belgian waffles with strawberries and whipped cream my family would eat every Easter brunch, or the cheesy potatoes served alongside the ham at Christmas dinner. Cinnamon rolls always remind my husband of Thanksgiving dinners in his grandma Helen's dining room. I've even carried on the tradition of baking a birthday cake for Baby Jesus every Christmas morning.

I love how the smell and sight of certain dishes (recipes for many of which are in this book) flood me with nostalgia. There are more than 100 recipes in *Surprise! It's Gluten-Free!*, and almost all of them have deeply-rooted ties to my family and friends—the incredible people who originally started making these (usually gluten-containing) recipes over the years. I've turned these tried-and-true dishes into gluten-free renditions. If you or someone for whom you cook has a gluten allergy or wants to change their eating habits, I gift these gluten-free recipes to you. I hope you find joy, tradition, and comfort in the same foods that are so important to me.

Cooking & Eating! They're in my Blood

I developed a love for cooking at a very young age. My mom was always whipping up yummy treats in the kitchen, whether it was a birthday, holiday, or a Sunday family dinner, and I loved spending days in the kitchen with her.

I can remember making peanut butter balls and rolling them in a dozen different toppings, or helping my mom to recreate family staples to be cholesterol-friendly for my father (and they tasted just like the amazing original recipes). Cooking was a bonding activity that always produced yummy results.

Not only do I love to cook anything and everything, but I have also always had a crazy love for eating any and all baked goods—cream puffs (my mom made the best ones), pies (again, mom's apple pie is the best), cakes (it's why I go to weddings), and donuts (oh my! *donuts!*). I was a child who always ordered waffles, or French toast, or cinnamon rolls, or anything that involved bread or dough for breakfast. For lunch and dinner, I always wanted pizza, pasta, rice, or anything with carbs as the main ingredient. I would go to certain restaurants because of the bread they served before the meal. Little did I know, all of these carbs had a grave effect on my body.

Mysterious Symptoms

For the first 22 years of my life, I had never heard the word "gluten." In my early twenties, I began to experience debilitating symptoms that affected my day-to-day experiences. I had no explanation for them and not the slightest idea they were tied to gluten, but they lasted for years. Severe anxiety, panic attacks, crippling gastrointestinal (GI) upset, daily headaches or migraines, constant canker sores, joint pain, persistent nausea, cramping, body aches, extreme fatigue, weight loss, and brain fog—they were my normal. I was afraid to go to sleep at night for fear of waking up an hour later, sick to my stomach. I even feared leaving my house after dinner, developing something called *agoraphobia*—an anxiety disorder characterized by an extreme fear of public places.

I sought medical help and underwent *so* many tests, none of which revealed any clear insight into what was wrong. When I started to stumble upon the foreign words "gluten" and "celiac" associated with a list of symptoms that matched my own, my doctors were dismissive. At the time, celiac disease and gluten sensitivity were poorly understood in the mainstream medical community, and as a result, I was lumped into the general diagnosis of irritable bowel syndrome (IBS) and told to try yoga and find other ways to relieve stress.

Over the years, anytime I thought I found the solution to my years of pain and uncertainty, more medications would be thrown my way and my symptoms would improve slightly, but I would still have bad flare-ups, receive a round of steroids, and start over.

As a young adult, I was barely able to manage my symptoms. I continued looking for answers, and every time I researched, I would come across gluten and celiac disease. Although my symptoms matched, my doctors would say, "No, that's not it." They also advised, "Don't give up gluten. In fact, eat more whole wheat. It's good for your colon."

I had decided that this was my life: weird diets, constant research, and the prospect that I would live the rest of my life feeling sick and defined by my anxiety.

No More Wheat?!

I remained resigned to what I had come to believe was my fate until I had kids. That changed everything, and I recommitted to fighting for my health. I wanted to be the "active mom," the "fun mom," and the "spontaneous mom." I had a mentor in my life at the time who was a nutritionist and natural wellness practitioner in town, so I set up an appointment with her, and the first thing she told me was to stop eating *gluten* (a term that was ever so slowly becoming a household word).

Oh my word! My life changed. My health changed! Within months, my headaches were gone, my heavy-feeling body was light, my foggy brain was clear, and all of my joint pain subsided. I'm still healing from years of damage, but my severe GI symptoms have gone away. My life definitely changed when I cut out gluten, and I never looked back.

Good Food, But Make It Gluten-Free

Going gluten-free was extremely difficult for me because of the centrality of food tradition in my life. However, the alternative (eating gluten and feeling awful) was so much worse than the lifestyle change. I know because I've "cheated" a few times and paid the price in misery.

I officially went gluten-free in 2008 when there were very few gluten-free alternatives on the grocery store shelves, and most restaurants had no clue how to accommodate a growing generation of gluten-free individuals. On the rare occasion I found gluten-free snacks or baked goods in a store, they were outrageously expensive, and I would often toss them out because they were so far from the tastes and textures I loved in their gluten-containing counterparts.

After spending unsustainable amounts of money on food I wasn't eating, I decided to use my love of cooking in a new way. My mother had bestowed on me such a strong culinary instinct, and I knew it was time to start experimenting and creating all the foods I was missing.

I can't tell you how many flour combinations I tried or how many loaves of bread or batches of cookies went straight into the trash can—if it tasted or looked gluten-free, then it was back to the drawing board. Eventually though, I got the hang of it. There are so many techniques and ingredients I've discovered throughout the process, and I'm really proud of the gluten-free dishes that have come out of my kitchen. If my personal taste testers—my family—are any testimony, then you could call my gluten-free creations a raving success.

The persistent experimentation turned into a small side business for me. I started baking for a few local stores and farmers markets in San Clemente, CA, and I started my own company, JF Bakes. Little did I know, my creations had a growing positive reputation around town. I started meeting strangers who found out I was the baker of "the best pumpkin bread" they'd ever had. Store owners wanted more of my goods on their shelves. I learned just how well-loved my baked goods were!

Turning the Page

My baking business grew fast (just like my two young boys) and I became overwhelmingly busy. I decided I couldn't juggle both the business and being the mom I wanted to be, so I shuttered my business. Shortly after, my older son Max was diagnosed with gluten sensitivity. This inspired me to keep cooking and creating because I wanted him to have all the same yummy meals and treats that every other child around him was enjoying.

One of the traditions at our Thanksgiving meal is Grandma Helen's Cinnamon Rolls. There was no way I was going to let those rolls get passed right underneath Max's nose without him enjoying one. So, I took up the task of creating a gluten-free cinnamon roll that he and I could both enjoy—and now you can too by following the recipe included in this book. The first few times we went to Disneyland after he became gluten-free, we would walk by the churro stands and inhale the heavenly smell of fried dough with cinnamon and sugar. So, the next day we would make churros and eat until our hearts and tummies were content. I never want my children to miss out on those food memories that last a lifetime.

When people ask me what my passions are, what makes me smile and get excited, it's easy to answer: seeing a child eat a cupcake, or a cookie, or a muffin for the very first time. I love when I create a dessert my son hasn't been able to eat in years and his face absolutely lights up when he takes his first bite. Or when someone is shocked that what they're eating is gluten-free—that's my passion.

That is why I'm writing this book. My hope is that the recipes in these pages enable you and your family and friends to enjoy delicious meals and treats with full confidence they support your health.

I want you to escape the hassle of cooking two of everything—one with gluten and one gluten-free. Now you can serve all of your family members and guests the same tasty home-cooked meals and desserts without one of them ever guessing that what they're eating is gluten-free. Please, just don't forget to say: "Surprise! It's gluten-free!"

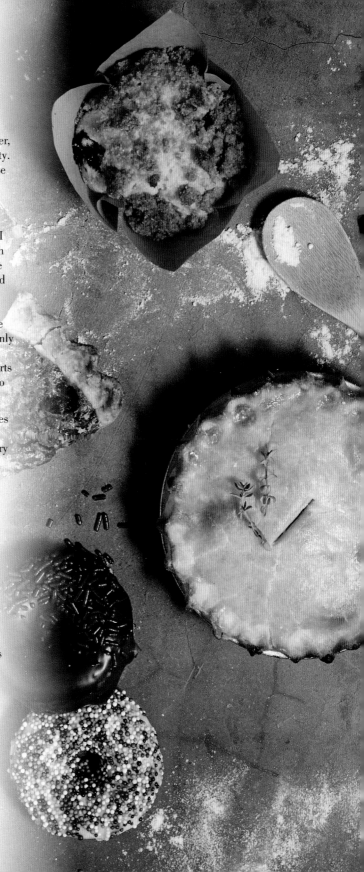

Gluten-Free Basics & Essential Flour Blends

The Big Deal with Gluten....................14

Secret Ingredients.........................16

Secret Techniques.........................20

The Blends................................24

The Big Deal with Gluten

Baking is a science that must be done precisely. If for health reasons you need to remove gluten from your baked goods, the scientific formula is even trickier, becoming more of an art form. There are no hard and fast rules for how to remove gluten-containing wheat (from your bread or cake, for instance) and still get the same structured, airy product you've always loved. However, we can look at all the ways that gluten makes your food amazing, compensate with alternative ingredients, and throw in a whole lot of trial and error in the test lab (kitchen!)—take a bite and you'd never know what was missing!

From Hero to Villain

Gluten is a protein that gives your baked goods structure, elasticity, and their light texture. When you use it in your batters and doughs, it creates little gas pockets and then acts like a miraculous net throughout the dough to trap the bubbles—resulting in the airy, beautiful crumb you see when you slice into a loaf. This effect can be difficult to replicate in gluten-free baking. Gluten would seem to many like an all-around win for producing amazing food, plus maybe you've always heard that grains are part of a healthy, balanced diet.

However, for those with celiac disease, gluten sensitivity, and other autoimmune conditions, the immune system is extremely sensitive to gluten. When someone with these illnesses consumes a food with gluten, their immune system goes into overdrive and begins to attack itself. This causes inflammation throughout the entire body, which leads to joint pain, skin reactions, gastrointestinal upset, nutritional deficiencies, and more. These are debilitating symptoms for many, and for those with celiac disease specifically, gluten causes long-term damage to the small intestine, making gluten a very disruptive villain to the body's systems.

The only way to eliminate the symptoms is to completely remove gluten from your diet. This is a significant lifestyle shift for many, but a worthwhile pursuit when you find your symptoms are managed or disappear. If gluten is disrupting your life like it did mine, it's likely time to plunge into the world of gluten-free alternatives. You probably already realized that store-bought gluten-free goods can be expensive and less delightful than their gluten-containing counterparts, so I'm excited to begin the process of gluten-free baking with you.

The Art of Gluten-Free Baking

When you remove gluten from the baking system, the main challenge is creating a product that isn't dense, dry, or gritty, or that sinks in the middle or crumbles to pieces upon the first bite. To make matters more difficult, the techniques and ingredients that work for one gluten-free recipe might not work well for the next. To imitate gluten, we add emulsifiers and stabilizers to the baking system, along with alternative proteins and starches. Ingredients such as rice flour, tapioca starch, eggs, vinegar, and gums can work together to create beautiful, bubbly, crumb-y baked goods that you'd never know were gluten-free! I have done all of the hard work for you with meticulously tested recipes that withstand the criticism of the most skeptical taste buds.

Once you start baking with gluten-free flours and living a gluten-free lifestyle, the easier it becomes. One of the easiest ways to always be prepared for gluten-free baking is to keep a large batch of my all-purpose gluten-free flour blends (page 24) on hand at all times. These will become your go-to flours. With many other secret tricks and ingredients, you'll learn to master this art form.

Gluten-Containing Grains

When you're avoiding gluten, you need to know all the foods that contain it. It's not just wheat flour that you need to watch out for. Gluten is the protein found in all wheat, rye, and barley. There are over 30,000 wheat varieties of 14 species grown throughout the world. Some of the more common varieties are spelt, farro, durum, kamut, bulgar, farina, semolina, and einkorn. Oats are also always in question. While they are naturally free of gluten, the problem arises with how they are often grown in the United States. When planted very close to wheat, cross-contamination can occur, which makes the oats irritating for many people. When you buy oats, always confirm they're certified gluten-free.

The same principle applies to all other packages: make sure you see an explicit certification of gluten-free; otherwise, you risk cross-contamination (which can be okay if your symptoms are more subtle, but will wreak havoc for individuals who are extremely sensitive).

Some products may have the label "wheat-free," but you need to confirm that it doesn't contain other forms of gluten from rye, barley, malt, or oats. You will soon learn that gluten is everywhere—salad dressings, sauces, spice mixes, marinades, and even cosmetics and other personal care products—but with practice, you'll learn how to read labels, ask questions, and discern whether a product is safe for you.

Secret Ingredients

Before you head into the kitchen to start baking your first batch of gluten-free goodies, read about the secret ingredients and other tips that make these recipes extra special. The specific ingredients I cover here help create fluffier baked goods that hold together well and will not crumble to pieces. I use these ingredients in almost every single one of my recipes to create a texture that leaves everyone questioning whether or not it is really gluten-free.

Flours

The million-dollar question: what do you use for flour when you can't use wheat flour? The answer is a blend of many different ingredients! You will not be able to use just one flour alternative (such as solely rice flour or solely almond flour) as a one-for-one substitute for wheat flour—you'll need to combine a few different grains and starches to reach your desired effect. I have created three different flour blends that use some combination of these ingredients: white and brown rice flour, tapioca flour, potato starch, arrowroot starch, sorghum flour, teff flour, and almond flour. I usually purchase organic Bob's Red Mill for all of these because I know they're certified gluten-free and of the highest quality, but you will likely have success with other brands.

- **Almond flour** is made from blanched almonds (not the same as almond meal, which is much coarser and contains the ground skins). It has a light, sweet flavor and keeps baked goods moist. Almond flour is low-carb, packed with nutrients, and high in fat and protein.

- **Arrowroot starch** (also called *arrowroot flour*) is an easily digested starch extracted from the arrowroot plant. Unlike most other starches, it's high in protein and several other nutrients.

- **Brown rice flour** is denser than other gluten-free flours, which is why it's best used in blends. It's ground from the whole grain, preserving the bran and germ from the rice kernel. It has a mild, nutty flavor. It's high in fiber, protein, and B vitamins.

- **Potato starch** adds moistness to gluten-free baking. It's the starch extracted from potatoes and is not the same thing as potato flour (which is flour ground from whole potatoes). This is also a great thickening agent for soups and sauces.

- **Sorghum flour** has a light color and texture with a mild sweet flavor. It's a good source of protein, iron, B vitamins, fiber, and antioxidants.

- **Tapioca flour** (also called *tapioca starch*) is a pure starch from the cassava root. It's excellent for thickening soups and sauces. It has a slightly sweet flavor.

- **Teff flour** works best when blended with other flours and starches because it has a very distinct flavor. It's high in calcium, protein, and iron, and it contains an excellent balance of amino acids.

- **White rice flour** imparts a slight sweetness to blends and a smooth texture.

Binders

I use xanthan gum in nearly all of my baked goods. It's a food additive produced by a microorganism called *Xanthomonas campestris*. Xanthan gum helps create elasticity in your dough and batter, acting as a gluten substitute to bind all of your ingredients together. Although xanthan gum is not absolutely necessary, without it, your baked goods will have a more crumbly texture and fall apart after they have been baked. I don't add xanthan gum to my premixed flour blends because I use different amounts in each recipe.

Note that large amounts of xanthan gum (anything over about 15g/0.5oz daily) may have a laxative effect or cause digestive discomfort. Most of my recipes use only 3 to 9 grams (0.1–0.3oz), and you're likely to consume only a few servings of any recipe in a given day. If you have digestive issues with xanthan gum, however, consider using an identical amount of guar gum (another thickening agent), instead. I have used both in my baking and have no preference for one over the other. My suggestion is to use whichever one your body tolerates best.

Eggs

Many of my recipes rely on eggs (always large ones). They are important for binding in gluten-free baking and help your recipes hold their structure. I use organic, pasture-raised eggs in my baking and cooking. You could substitute flax eggs or other egg substitutes if you're sensitive to eggs, but these will not yield the same outcome and may cause your baked goods to crumble.

Leavening Agents

Baking powder increases the volume and lightens up your baked goods—perfect for when you're working with gluten-free flours. I always use aluminum-free versions. A few of my recipes call for baking soda as well as baking powder, but because baking soda requires acid to activate, it's only included in recipes with a higher acid content. Always check the expiration dates of your baking powder and soda.

Sugars

You'll notice I always call for pure cane sugar, which is all natural, unrefined, and non-GMO. Unlike refined sugar, pure cane sugar isn't pure white in color and the crystals are a bit larger. You're welcome to substitute with refined white sugar, but it may not always yield the exact same result.

You can substitute coconut sugar in any recipe, cup-for-cup. Maple sugar may be substituted as well, however it's twice as sweet as pure cane sugar, so you may need to experiment to get to a sweetness level you prefer. I don't recommend using honey or maple syrup in place of pure cane sugar; the wet to dry ingredient ratio will be out of balance and may not produce a good result.

Apple Cider Vinegar

If you've ever picked up a loaf of gluten-free bread or a gluten-free cake, you might have noticed it's quite heavy. Gluten-free baked goods tend to be very dense, but apple cider vinegar helps lighten them up. When mixed with baking soda, it creates carbon dioxide gas (tiny air bubbles) in your dough, which creates fluffier, lighter dough that will rise a little better and not fall flat. I always use apple cider vinegar that contains the mother, the active enzyme component of the vinegar that makes it look a little cloudy but imparts many health benefits. I recommend you also always choose a raw, unfiltered vinegar that contains the mother, or your results may differ.

Butter

Any salted butter will work, but my favorite is Kerrygold Pure Irish Butter because it's organic and made from the milk of grass-fed cows. In any of my recipes that call for salted butter, consider using a high-quality butter such as this one, if it's available, because it makes a notable difference in elevating the flavors of your baking.

Maintaining Your Gluten-Free Diet

Beginning a gluten-free diet can be daunting and may seem impossible, but I promise it gets easier with time. I don't give it a second thought anymore because it's so much a part of how I live. Here are my top tips for success:

- **READ LABELS!** Gluten is sneaky.

- **FULLY STOCK YOUR GLUTEN-FREE KITCHEN.** Always have a gluten-free flour blend prepared and stored in the refrigerator. Other helpful staples are gluten-free condiments, gluten-free pasta, and chicken stock. Tamari (a gluten-free soy sauce) or coconut aminos are great soy sauce substitutes to have on hand.

- **NEVER ASSUME A MENU ITEM IS GLUTEN-FREE.** Always alert your server to your allergy. Many people are so sensitive they can't eat anything that has been fried in the same oil that was used for a product containing gluten. For example, I can only eat French fries or tortilla chips if they have been fried in their own oil—not oil used for chicken tenders, corn dogs, or any item containing gluten.

- **CARRY SNACKS EVERYWHERE YOU GO.** I usually have gluten-free crackers, an apple, or a beef stick in my purse.

- **CHECK YOUR PERSONAL CARE PRODUCTS.** Not everyone is sensitive to this, but if you are, double-check every product. (It's surprising how much shampoo actually rinses down your face and into your mouth!) If you're eating gluten-free and not seeing relief in your symptoms, this is the next place to check.

- **BE CAREFUL OF CROSS-CONTAMINATION.** If you're sharing a kitchen where gluten is used, be careful of your surfaces and utensils. For example, don't stir a pot of whole wheat spaghetti and then use the same spoon to stir your gluten-free pasta. Also, flour travels through the air very easily. If wheat flour was previously used in your kitchen, be sure to clean any work surfaces, utensils, or appliances before making anything gluten-free.

- **CHECK YOUR MEDICATIONS.** Gluten is often used as a binder in medications or in the capsules.

- **TRY TO COOK AT HOME AS MUCH AS POSSIBLE.** Not only is it safer because you know exactly what is in your food, but it will help your wallet, too. Gluten-free foods can be very expensive, especially when eating out. You will almost always notice an upcharge when substituting a gluten-free bun or pizza dough.

- **DON'T CHEAT!** A gluten-free diet is unlike any other diet; you can't have a "cheat day" every so often, or you will not find relief from your symptoms. Gluten stays in your body for a long time. For example, if I accidentally consume gluten, it often takes 2 to 3 weeks before I feel normal again. If you notice you're not getting any better on a gluten-free diet, make sure you're not accidentally consuming gluten somewhere—even the smallest amounts can affect sensitive individuals.

- **IF YOUR FAMILY IS SUPPORTIVE, MAKE YOUR WHOLE HOUSE GLUTEN-FREE.** (We've done this in my house even though only two out of four of us must avoid gluten.) First, this makes life easier. It can be very taxing to cook multiple meals every day. Second, it helps you to avoid any cross-contamination. I don't want any wheat flour touching my appliances. Third, it's cheaper. Buying many versions of breads, pastas, or crackers can be very expensive. Finally, it improves your gluten-free cooking skills!

Using Store-Bought 1-to-1 Flour Blends

Page 24 shares the flour blends I use in every recipe in this book. If you don't have the time or desire to mix up these blends, you may use a store-bought blend that is already created for you. When selecting a store-bought blend, look for something that is the most similar to one of my blends. I cannot guarantee you'll arrive at the same final product, but they should work. However, substituting straight rice flour or oat flour (or any singular type of flour) will not work. In order to create the elasticity, structure, and proper texture, you need a certain percent of starch combined with the flours. Blends always work the best!

Other Fats & Oils

I often use palm shortening in my baking, which creates a tender inside and a crispy outside. However, not all palm shortenings are created the same. The amount of water can vary between brands of palm shortenings, which can cause your baked goods to come out different from what's intended. For instance, if you use a brand with a higher water content, your dozen cookies could spread into one mega-cookie! I always use Spectrum palm shortening and recommend that you use it as well. If you are not able to find this brand, try using butter instead, or refrigerating your shortening and your dough before baking.

For cooking and baking with oil, avocado oil is my favorite. It has a very light flavor and the highest smoke point of all plant-based oils; unlike other oils, it won't oxidate under heat, which is toxic for your body.

Store-Bought Pasta

I use Tinkyada brand, if possible. If I can't find this brand, then I will use any variety of 100 percent brown rice pasta, which I've found is the most similar to wheat pasta; it holds its shape and has the best texture. In my experience, pastas that include corn or other grains tend to crumble or can be crunchy, especially if not eaten immediately.

I have two tips for cooking with gluten-free pasta. First, never cook as long as the package says to; I usually start tasting the pasta 3 to 4 minutes prior to the package's recommended cooking time. Second, rinse the pasta under water immediately after cooking. This will wash off the starches and help prevent the pasta from becoming slimy and mushy. The recipe will specify if you need to use hot or cold water.

Milk

I use organic whole milk or canned full-fat coconut milk in most of my recipes that call for milk. You can substitute almond milk, rice milk, or full-fat canned coconut milk in place of cow's milk in any recipe. Some recipes call for canned coconut cream, which is the solid, thicker part of the full-fat canned coconut milk, but you can substitute heavy whipping cream.

Secret Techniques

Gluten-free baking is often a lot of trial and error. Fortunately, I've done all the trial and error for you. If you follow recipe directions precisely, measure ingredients properly, and use the suggested brands, you too can have baked goods that taste just like the gluten-filled originals!

Measuring

Careful measuring, especially of flour, is very important. I never use my measuring cup to scoop flour directly from the container. If you do this, you're more likely to use too much flour, which will produce a drier, denser product. Always use a separate tool to scoop flour from the container and pour into the measuring cup. Overfill the measuring cup, and then level off with a knife. You don't need to sift the flours in a recipe unless it's specifically instructed.

Greasing

You'll notice most of my recipes instruct you to only grease the bottom of the pan (not the sides). Gluten-free baked goods need all the help they can get to get a proper rise, and the sides of the pan help. The sides of pans give doughs and batters something to stick to, helping your baked goods keep their risen shape. If the sides are greased, the dough tends to pull away from the sides and then fall. Once your baked goods are cooled, if the food needs a little bit of coaxing out of the pan, you can gently run a butter knife around the perimeter.

Mixing Time

Because there is no gluten in your dough, in general you don't need to be cautious of overmixing (i.e., overdeveloping the gluten) or undermixing. However, there are still some instances where mixing time is important. For instance, if you overmix scones or biscuits, they will not be flaky. If you overmix a recipe with whipped egg whites, the mix could deflate. For recipes with yeast, you need a few minutes of extra mixing (which takes the place of kneading). For the best success, always follow the instructions in the recipe.

Kneading Doughs

Gluten-free doughs are very different from doughs with gluten, especially bread doughs. They will be much stickier and thinner, and you won't be able to knead a gluten-free dough as you would a dough containing gluten. My recipes all call for "kneading" your dough using a stand mixer with the paddle attachment. The doughs are too thin and sticky for the hook attachment.

Flouring Your Surfaces

Because the doughs are so much stickier, anytime you place the dough on a surface, it's very important that you've floured it properly. I almost always use parchment paper as a base, and I usually use tapioca flour when flouring surfaces; it tends to work the best in preventing sticking to the surface and it also blends in nicely with the dough. It will not leave a gritty layer on the final product like rice flour would. You could also use your flour blend, but there is a slight risk of drying the mixture out too much.

Freshness of Ingredients

Fresh ingredients are critical and may be the reason for a failed outcome. For example, baking powder is used to create rise and lighten the texture of your baked goods; expired baking powder could cause a cake or muffin to sink in the middle. The same thing is true of baking soda, yeast, and eggs.

Temperature of Ingredients

Some recipes call for firm (chilled), softened, or room temperature butter, eggs, or palm shortening. It's critical to follow the directions when it specifically mentions what temperature your ingredients should be, or your final product may not turn out as it should, often related to excessive spreading. When a recipe uses yeast, it is likewise very important to add your warm water within the specified temperature range or the yeast might not activate.

Baking in Batches

When baking cookies, muffins, scones, and anything on a cookie or baking sheet, only cook one sheet at a time, in the middle of your oven, with the items properly spaced on that sheet. Your baked goods won't cook evenly if the oven is overcrowded. For most of my baked good recipes, you'll need to bake in batches. However, gluten-free batters tend to be fluffier the longer the batter sits, so cooking in batches is usually a good thing. (The muffins or cupcakes from the last batch always have the best crown on them because they get to sit the longest before going in the oven!) Keep an eye out, though, for certain recipes that require refrigeration between batches.

Allowing Batters & Doughs to Rest

Resting the doughs allows the flours and starches to absorb moisture, which will soften your mixture and create more of a rise in your baked goods. You'll get the best structure and shape if you always follow instructions for resting (and sometimes refrigerating or freezing) your doughs.

Cooling

Because gluten-free goods tend to be a bit more delicate than their counterparts, you'll often see instructions to cool your food on or in the pan instead of removing the food to a rack. Do not rush or skip this part! Removing a baked good from the pan too quickly may result in a pile of crumbs or a sunken disappointment.

Read the Entire Recipe Before Starting

Some recipes call for ingredients at room temperature or chilling before baking. For example, you don't want to start a cookie recipe that you plan to have for dessert right after dinner and then realize the dough needs to chill for at least 2 hours!

Storing Your Foods

Fresh gluten-free baked goods tend to dry out much faster than a gluten- or preservative-filled item, and refrigeration often accelerates the drying out process. I very rarely suggest storing your items in the refrigerator. Gluten-free items are best stored in the freezer. The freezer helps retain the moisture and prevents them from drying out. However, it is very important that your items are placed in an airtight container or freezer bag first. I typically like to separate each serving with parchment paper or plastic wrap, as well.

Troubleshooting

Here are some common errors and how to address them.

- **NO "CROWN" ON YOUR MUFFINS, CAKES, CUPCAKES:** There are many factors to consider. Check the freshness of baking powder and soda. If flour is under-measured and you have too much liquid in a mixture, increase the flour 1 tablespoon at a time. An oven that is too hot can cause the item to set before the bubbles have formed a rise; if the oven is too cold, the item will rise too quickly and then fall before the center is set. You need a slow and consistent rise, so always preheat the oven thoroughly, and consider double-checking the accuracy of the oven's temperature with a separate oven thermometer. If butter or shortening is too soft, refrigerate the batter before baking to help the food rise up when in the oven instead of melting down.

- **DRY OR CRUMBLY:** If you over-measured your flour, add liquid 1 to 2 tablespoons at a time. If you didn't use xanthan gum when it was called for, it may cause crumbliness. Overcooking will also yield a drier final product.

- **GUMMY OR DENSE:** If gummy, you may have used too much xanthan gum. (But hopefully my trial and error for all my recipes has prevented denseness!) If you're still having trouble, check the freshness on your baking powder or soda, or use a tad bit more. Omitting the apple cider vinegar will also lead to a more dense product.

- **ALTITUDE ADJUSTMENTS:** Baking at higher altitudes can be difficult, particularly when you throw "gluten-free" into the mix. I've found that the following tips will help create a great final product. (1) Increase the oven temperature by 15°F (10°C), and decrease the baking time by 5 to 8 minutes. (2) Increase the flour by 1 tablespoon per cup. (3) Decrease the sugar by 1 tablespoon per cup. (4) Increase the liquid by 1 to 2 tablespoons (or add 1 additional egg white). (5) Decrease the baking powder and soda. (This part is tricky; KingArthurBaking.com has posted a very helpful leavening adjustment chart that I use.)

- **MUSHY IN THE MIDDLE:** Your food was either not cooked long enough or had too much liquid in the batter.

- **SPREADING EXCESSIVELY:** You either have too much liquid in the dough, or your dough needs to be refrigerated before baking.

The Blends

Whip up a batch or two of my amazing flour blends and keep in the fridge, making gluten-free baking a cinch. My favorite is the #1 All-Purpose Flour Blend, which tends to be very forgiving, but the #2 All-Purpose Flour Blend is great for sensitive tummies. The Ancient Grain Flour Blend is ideal for when you have a fancy for something that tastes whole grain.

#1 All-Purpose Flour Blend

This is the flour blend I use most often. I make a large batch of it and store it in an airtight container in my refrigerator. It can easily replace white flour in almost any recipe cup-for-cup. I also use this blend if a recipe calls for flour to thicken a sauce or gravy. It is a great all-purpose flour.

Yield: about 4¾ cups

300g (about 2 cups) white rice flour
200g (about 1½ cups) brown rice flour
100g (about ¾ cup) tapioca flour
75g (about ½ cup) potato starch

#2 All-Purpose Flour Blend

This is another all-purpose blend that I use in a few of my recipes. It's made without brown rice flour. I almost always use my #1 All-Purpose Flour Blend, but if you do not digest brown rice very well, then use this brown rice–free version as a substitute in any recipe.

Yield: about 4 cups

500g (about 3 cups) white rice flour
110g (about ⅔ cup) potato starch
35g (about ¼ cup) arrowroot starch
70g (about ½ cup) tapioca flour

Ancient Grain Flour Blend

Unlike modern wheat, corn, and white rice, ancient grains are a grouping of crops that haven't been changed (or only very slightly altered) by selective breeding. This blend is a great whole wheat flour replacement. It has a higher protein, fiber, antioxidant, and vitamin content than my other two flour blends. It's also moister than the other blends and may require longer cooking times. The final product is typically a bit denser.

Yield: about 7¾ cups

200g (about 1¾ cups) sorghum flour
300g (about 2¼ cups) brown rice flour
200g (about 1½ cups) teff flour
125g (about 1 cup) arrowroot starch
175g (about 1¼ cups) tapioca flour

For any of the blends, in a large bowl, whisk or sift all of the flours thoroughly to combine, making sure the blend is evenly mixed.

Store it

Store in an airtight container at room temperature for 1 to 2 months, in the refrigerator for 4 to 6 months, or in the freezer for up to 1 year.

Tip

I recommend using a scale to measure out the different flours. While not necessary, it's the best way to create an accurate blend. If you don't have a scale, be sure to pour the flour into your measuring cup with a separate spoon and level off the measuring cup with a knife. (If you scoop the flour using your measuring cup, you will most likely pack in too much flour, and it will not create an accurate blend.)

Homemade Breadcrumbs

I have used many different brands of store-bought gluten-free breadcrumbs over the years. Some have been fantastic and some not good at all. The problems I have run into are always related to texture: they are either very dry and hard, or they can be the exact opposite and turn mushy as soon as they come into contact with any moisture. When in a hurry, store-bought gluten-free breadcrumbs will work in any of my recipes, but if you have the time, homemade breadcrumbs create better texture and flavor. They are very easy to make and store very well in an airtight container in the freezer. So, before you throw out any stale gluten-free bread, use it to make breadcrumbs and then toss them in your freezer, ready for use at any time.

Yield: about ¾ cup

4 slices of gluten-free bread

1. Preheat the oven to 350°F (180°C). Cut the bread slices into 1-inch (2.5cm) cubes. Arrange the cubes in a single layer on a baking sheet.

2. Bake for 15 minutes. If the bread is still soft at all, continue to bake for an additional 5 to 10 minutes, checking often to make sure they don't burn.

3. Cool the bread cubes and then pulse in a food processor until fine crumbs are formed.

Store it

Store in an airtight container in the freezer for up to 6 months.

Tip

Use your favorite store-bought gluten-free bread, or use homemade bread. Good options from this book include the Easy White Sandwich Bread (page 113), the Ancient Grain Sandwich Bread (page 112), Traditional English Muffins (page 31), and Hamburger Buns (page 116). I like to collect all of the ends and small pieces of bread that no one eats and keep them in a bag in the freezer. Once I've collected a good amount, I use them to make breadcrumbs.

Wheat-Free Mornings

Chewy Granola Bars.............................28

Almond Granola.................................30

Traditional English Muffins...............31

Fluffy Pancakes................................33

Ancient Grain Waffles......................34

Belgian Waffle Wannabes.................35

Grandma Helen's Cinnamon Rolls.......36

Flaky Sour Cream Biscuits.................38

Cream-Filled Donuts.........................39

Donuts 5 Ways..................................41

Makes:
18–24

Prep time:
10 minutes

Cook time:
30 minutes

My oat bars (page 176)—which are nothing short of a crowd-pleaser and are definitely a dessert—inspired this lightly sweetened breakfast recipe. I had a few friends ask me to create a healthier version of the oat bars, so I created these granola bars, which do not contain any refined sugar and are full of yummy, healthy ingredients.

Chewy Granola Bars

1 cup sliced raw almonds

¼ cup raw sunflower seeds

¼ cup raw pepitas

2 cups old-fashioned rolled oats (certified gluten-free)

¼ cup unsweetened shredded coconut

½ cup #1 All-Purpose Flour Blend (page 24) or Ancient Grain Flour Blend (page 24)

½ tsp xanthan gum

½ tsp ground cinnamon

3 tbsp salted butter

¼ cup honey

⅓ cup pure maple syrup

¼ cup coconut sugar

1½ tsp pure vanilla extract

¼ tsp salt

½ cup finely chopped pitted dates

½ cup finely chopped dried apricots (unsulfured and unsweetened)

½ cup dried cranberries or raisins

1. Preheat the oven to 350°F (180°C) and line the bottom of an 8 x 12-inch (20 x 30.5cm) or 9 x 13-inch (23 x 33cm) baking dish with parchment paper.

2. Put the almonds, sunflower seeds, and pepitas in a food processor and pulse a few times, just enough to chop them up a little bit.

3. In a large bowl, stir together the chopped nuts and seeds, oats, and coconut. Spread the mixture out onto a baking sheet. Bake for 10 to 12 minutes, stirring occasionally, until lightly toasted.

4. Transfer to a large bowl and mix in the #1 All-Purpose Flour Blend, xanthan gum, and cinnamon. Reduce the oven temperature to 300°F (150°C).

5. In a small saucepan, stir together the butter, honey, maple syrup, coconut sugar, vanilla, and salt, and bring to a boil over medium heat. Once it starts to boil, cook, stirring constantly, for 1 minute.

6. Pour the hot mixture over the oatmeal mixture. Add the chopped dates, apricots, and cranberries, and stir well. Spread the mixture into the parchment-lined baking pan and press down until evenly spread. (Wet your fingers to prevent the mixture from sticking to your hands.)

7. Bake for 20 to 25 minutes or until starting to turn light golden brown. Cool in the pan for at least 2 to 3 hours before cutting into 3-inch (7.5cm) long bars.

Tips

Refrigerate the dates and apricots for a few hours before making these bars. It'll make them easier to cut.

If you have a hard time digesting nuts or seeds, you can soak them in filtered water for about 4 hours before starting this recipe. Soaked nuts and seeds are more easily digested.

Mix it up with your choice of dried fruits or nuts. For example, replace the dates, cranberries, or apricots with dried apples, cherries, blueberries, pineapple, etc.

For extra sweetness, drizzle melted chocolate on top of the cooled bars.

Store it

Store in an airtight container on the counter for up to 5 days or in the freezer for up to 3 months. Thaw at room temperature.

Makes:
about 6 cups

Prep time:
10 minutes

Cook time:
1 hour

I developed this lightly sweet, crunchy, nut-filled granola when I was looking for a healthier option containing more than just oats. When I was baking and selling to a few local stores, it quickly became a customer favorite. It's great with ice cream or as the topping on an apple or berry crisp.

Almond Granola

1¼ cups sliced raw almonds

¾ cup raw sunflower seeds

¾ cup raw pepitas

1¾ cups old-fashioned rolled oats (certified gluten-free)

¾ cup unsweetened shredded coconut

1 tsp ground cinnamon

½ tsp salt

⅓ cup coconut oil, melted

⅓ cup raw honey

¼ cup filtered water

1 tsp pure vanilla extract

1. Preheat the oven to 300°F (150°C) and line a large rimmed baking sheet with parchment paper. In a large bowl, combine the almonds, sunflower seeds, pepitas, oats, shredded coconut, cinnamon, and salt.

2. Add the melted coconut oil to the items in the bowl and stir to evenly coat. Warm the honey in the microwave for about 20 seconds, and then add to the mixture and stir to evenly coat.

3. In a small bowl, stir together the water and vanilla. Add to the granola and stir until well combined. Evenly spread the granola on the baking sheet, spreading it to the edges and leveling it as much as possible.

4. Bake for 45 to 55 minutes, stirring the granola every 10 minutes for the first 30 minutes, and then every 5 minutes for the remaining cooking time. Be sure to smooth the granola back out after each stir. The granola is done when it turns golden brown. Cool completely on the pan. Serve at room temperature.

Store it

Store in an airtight container on the counter for up to 2 weeks or in the freezer for up to 3 months. Thaw at room temperature.

Makes:
6

Prep time:
1 hour, plus 45 minutes
to rise

Cook time:
35 minutes

Any kind of toasted bread with butter is my favorite morning snack, and these English muffins fit the bill! Don't let the number of cooking steps overwhelm you; they're actually really easy to make. Prepare a double batch and keep some in the freezer!

Traditional English Muffins

1⅓ cups whole milk
1 tbsp pure cane sugar
1 tsp salt
1 tbsp salted butter
2 tsp apple cider vinegar
¾ cup white rice flour
½ cup tapioca flour
1 cup Ancient Grain Flour Blend
   (page 24)
2 tsp xanthan gum
2¼ tsp rapid-rise yeast
½ cup blanched almond flour,
   to sprinkle
Cooking spray, to coat

1. In a small saucepan, combine the milk, sugar, salt, and butter over low heat. Stir until the sugar is dissolved. Transfer the mixture to a stand mixer fitted with the paddle attachment or a large bowl. Let cool to 105 to 110°F (40–43°C). Once the milk reaches the specified temperature range, stir in the vinegar.

2. While the milk mixture is cooling, sift together the rice flour, tapioca flour, Ancient Grain Flour Blend, xanthan gum, and yeast. Add the flour blend to the milk, and beat on low speed until well incorporated. Scrape down the sides of the bowl. Beat again on medium-high speed for 3 minutes. The dough will be very sticky. Cover and set aside in a warm place to rise for 30 to 45 minutes or until doubled in size. When the batter is done rising, gently stir the dough with a spatula to deflate.

3. While the dough is rising, preheat the oven to 350°F (180°C). During the last 5 minutes of rising, heat a griddle pan on the stove over medium-low heat or set an electric griddle to 325° (170°C). Lightly oil the pan. Spray the insides of 6 English muffin rings with cooking spray and set close together on the warm griddle.

4. Sprinkle about 1 teaspoon almond flour onto the griddle inside each ring. Using a lightly greased ⅓ cup measuring cup, place a heaping scoop of dough into each ring. Spray the top of each muffin with cooking spray. Place a piece of parchment paper over the rings and lightly press the dough down with a spoon to smooth. Remove the paper. Sprinkle about 1 teaspoon almond flour on top of each muffin. Then place the parchment paper back on top. Place a sheet pan on top of the parchment-covered rings to prevent them from rising too much.

Store it ···············

These muffins freeze very well without drying out. Split the muffins apart before freezing, then put them back together and individually wrap in plastic wrap. Freeze in an airtight container. When ready to eat, you can either place directly into the toaster, thaw at room temperature, or microwave for 20 to 30 seconds.

5. Cook on the stove for 4 to 6 minutes or until lightly golden brown on the bottom. Uncover and use two spatulas to flip the rings. Re-cover with the paper and sheet pan, and cook for another 4 to 6 minutes. Transfer the rings from the griddle to the parchment-lined sheet pan and bake in the oven for 3 minutes. Remove the rings from the muffins, place a new piece of parchment paper on top of the muffins, along with a sheet pan if needed to prevent the paper from curling. Bake for 15 minutes more, or until the edges spring back when pinched.

6. Cool on a wire rack for 10 to 15 minutes. When cool enough to touch, use a fork to perforate the muffin all around the perimeter (but do not yet split or cut through). The dough will be very gooey on the inside, and you will need to clean your fork throughout the process. When ready to eat, cut the English muffin in half and toast. It can be used for eggs Benedict or topped with butter, jelly, almond butter, or your favorite topping.

Makes:
1 dozen (3-in/
7.5cm) pancakes

Prep time:
10 minutes

Cook time:
10 minutes

My children would eat pancakes every single morning if I put a stack in front of them. Creating a super yummy wheat-free pancake recipe was a must. I love serving them to people who aren't gluten-conscious because they have no idea they are gluten-free!

Fluffy Pancakes

1 cup whole milk, plus more to thin

1 tbsp fresh lemon juice

1 cup #1 All-Purpose Flour Blend (page 24)

1 tsp xanthan gum

2 tbsp pure cane sugar

1 tsp baking powder

½ tsp baking soda

½ tsp salt

1 large egg

1 tsp pure vanilla extract

2 tbsp salted butter, melted and cooled

Palm shortening or coconut oil, to grease

1. In a small bowl, whisk together the milk and lemon juice and set aside for 5 minutes to sour.

2. In a large bowl, whisk together the #1 All-Purpose Flour Blend, xanthan gum, sugar, baking powder, baking soda, and salt.

3. In a separate medium bowl, slightly whisk the egg. Whisk in the vanilla, soured milk, and melted butter. Pour the milk mixture into the flour mixture and whisk until smooth.

4. Heat a nonstick griddle pan over medium heat, and then grease it with palm shortening or coconut oil. Ladle ¼-cup portions of batter onto the preheated skillet and cook 1 to 2 minutes or until golden brown on the bottom. Flip and cook until golden brown on the other side. (Pancake batter may thicken as it sits. If it gets too thick to work with, you can add small amounts of milk, 1 tablespoon at a time, to thin it out.)

5. Serve immediately with butter, chocolate chips, pure maple syrup, fresh berries or banana slices, walnuts, or powdered sugar.

Store it

Cool on a wire rack. Place in an airtight container with parchment paper separating the pancakes. Freeze for up to 3 months. When ready to eat, place directly into the toaster.

Tips

The lemon juice is the secret to the fluffiness of these pancakes. The acid reacts with the baking soda, creating tiny air bubbles that fluff up the batter.

To make these a bit healthier, prepare a version using the Ancient Grain Flour Blend. For the flour, use ¾ cup Ancient Grain Flour Blend (page 24) and ¼ cup #1 All-Purpose Flour Blend (page 24). Replace the pure cane sugar with coconut sugar.

These are great breakfast waffles to eat before heading out to school or work. They are full of nutrient-dense grains and oats. Keep a large batch in the freezer and pop them into the toaster in the morning to reheat. Greasing the waffle iron with palm shortening is a must to create the crispy outer layer.

Ancient Grain Waffles

Melted palm shortening,
    to grease
1½ cups Ancient Grain Flour
    Blend (page 24)
¼ cup blanched almond flour
1 tsp xanthan gum
3 tbsp coconut sugar or
    maple sugar
¼ cup old-fashioned rolled oats
    (certified gluten-free)
2 tsp baking powder
1 tsp salt
½ tsp baking soda
1½ cups whole milk
2 tsp apple cider vinegar
1 tsp pure vanilla extract
3 tbsp salted butter, melted
    and cooled
2 large eggs, separated

1. Preheat the waffle iron according to manufacturer's instructions and lightly brush with palm shortening.

2. In a large bowl, whisk together the Ancient Grain Flour Blend, almond flour, xanthan gum, coconut sugar, oats, baking powder, salt, and baking soda until thoroughly combined.

3. In a medium bowl, whisk together the milk, vinegar, vanilla, and butter. Separate the egg whites into a separate medium bowl, and add the yolks to the milk-butter mixture. Whisk the milk-yolk mixture until well combined. Whisk the wet ingredients into the dry ingredients until just combined, but do not overmix.

4. Beat the egg whites until soft peaks form. Gently fold the egg whites into the batter.

5. Ladle the batter into the prepared waffle iron and cook according to the manufacturer's instructions. These waffles tend to spread out, so do not fill too full or manually spread out the batter too much. Brush more palm shortening onto the waffle iron between batches. Serve warm with butter, maple syrup, or fresh fruit.

Store it

Let the waffles cool completely on a wire rack. Place in an airtight container with parchment paper separating the waffles. Freeze for up to 3 months. When ready to eat, place directly into the toaster.

Yield:
5–6

Prep time:
20 minutes

Cook time:
15 minutes

Growing up, we would have Belgian waffles with strawberries and homemade whipped cream every Easter morning, so a good homemade waffle recipe was an absolute must! Your morning guests will never guess that these are gluten-free.

Belgian Waffle Wannabes

Melted palm shortening, to grease
2 tbsp fresh lemon juice
2 cups whole milk
2 cups #1 All-Purpose Flour Blend (page 24)
1 tsp xanthan gum
2 tbsp pure cane sugar
2 tsp baking powder
1 tsp baking soda
½ tsp salt
3 large eggs, separated
⅓ cup salted butter, melted and cooled
1 tsp pure vanilla extract

Whipped Cream (optional)

1 cup heavy whipping cream
1–3 tbsp pure maple syrup (depending on desired sweetness)

1. Preheat the waffle iron according to the manufacturer's instructions and lightly brush with palm shortening. In a medium bowl, whisk together the lemon juice and milk, and set aside to sour.

2. In large bowl, whisk together the #1 All-Purpose Flour Blend, xanthan gum, sugar, baking powder, baking soda, and salt until combined.

3. Separate the egg whites into a separate medium bowl, and add the yolks to the soured milk, along with the melted butter and vanilla. Whisk until well combined and frothy. Add the milk mixture to flour mixture, and whisk until well combined.

4. Beat the egg whites until soft peaks form. Gently fold the egg whites into the batter.

5. Ladle the batter into the prepared waffle iron and cook according to the manufacturer's instructions. Brush more palm shortening onto the waffle iron between batches. Serve warm with butter, maple syrup, or strawberries and homemade whipped cream (if desired).

Whipped Cream: In a stand mixer fitted with the whisk attachment or in a medium bowl, beat the cream with the maple syrup until stiff peaks form.

Store it

Let the waffles cool completely on a wire rack. Place in an airtight container with parchment paper separating the waffles. Freeze for up to 3 months. When ready to eat, place directly into the toaster.

Tip

For some added protein, add 1 serving of grass-fed beef collagen to the dry ingredients.

Makes:
8–9

Prep time:
30 minutes, plus
2 hours to rise

Cook time:
25 minutes

These cinnamon rolls are a tradition at my husband's family Thanksgiving. We made a trip to see 92-year-old Grandma Helen, and she showed me how it's done! I adapted her recipe to be gluten-free, and now we all get to enjoy Grandma Helen's rolls every holiday.

Grandma Helen's Cinnamon Rolls

1½ cups #1 All-Purpose Flour Blend (page 24)

1¼ cups sorghum flour

½–¾ cup tapioca flour, plus more to flour

2¼ tsp rapid-rise yeast

2 tsp xanthan gum

1 tsp salt

1 tsp unflavored gelatin

¼ cup salted butter, softened

½ cup pure cane sugar

2 large eggs

1 cup warm water (105–110°F/40–43°C)

1 tbsp apple cider vinegar

Filling

¼ cup salted butter, melted

½ cup firmly packed light brown sugar

2 tsp ground cinnamon

Icing (optional)

1 cup powdered sugar

½ tsp pure vanilla extract

2–2½ tbsp whole milk

1. Lightly grease only the bottom of an 8- or 9-inch (20 or 23cm) square baking pan. In a medium bowl, stir together the #1 All-Purpose Flour Blend, sorghum flour, ½ cup tapioca flour, yeast, xanthan gum, salt, and gelatin.

2. In a stand mixer fitted with the paddle attachment or in a large bowl, cream together the butter and sugar on medium-high speed until light and fluffy. Add the eggs one at a time, blending well on high speed after each addition. Add the warm water and vinegar and blend on medium speed until combined.

3. Slowly add the flour mixture to the wet ingredients and beat on low speed until combined. Increase the speed to medium-high and beat for 2 minutes. (The dough will be very sticky. If it's too sticky or runny to get out of the bowl, add more tapioca flour 1 tablespoon at a time, but do not add more than ¼ cup.)

4. Heavily dust a 2-foot (0.5m) long piece of parchment paper with tapioca flour. Wet your hands with warm water and spread the dough over the length and width of the parchment paper, making it 18 to 19 inches (45–48cm) long and about ⅛ to ¼-inch (3–5mm) thick. Continue to wet your hands while pressing out the dough to prevent sticking.

5. For the filling, brush the melted butter over the dough from edge to edge. In a small bowl, combine the brown sugar and cinnamon. Sprinkle over the dough from edge to edge.

6. Starting at the short end and using the parchment as a guide, very carefully roll up the dough as tightly as possible. Patch any holes by squeezing the dough together. Using a sharp knife dipped in tapioca flour, cut the roll into 9 equally sized disks, and place the disks into the prepared baking dish. (It is okay if they are crowded or touching.) Let the rolls rise in a warm place for 1 to 2 hours or until almost doubled in size. Once the rolls are almost done rising, preheat the oven to 375°F (190°C).

7. Bake for 20 to 25 minutes or until starting to turn golden brown. Cool in the pan until the butter stops bubbling, and then flip them out onto a plate. Serve warm with butter, or drizzle icing over the top.

   Icing: In a small bowl, stir together the powdered sugar, vanilla, and 2 tablespoons whole milk. Add additional milk 1 teaspoon at a time as needed until a smooth, thin icing is formed.

Store it

Store in an airtight container in the freezer for up to 3 months. Thaw at room temperature or reheat in the microwave.

Tips

The dough will not be like a gluten-containing cinnamon roll dough; it will be very sticky and a little difficult to work with. Do not use a rolling pin to roll out the dough. Wet hands are the best way to spread it out. The parchment paper for rolling the dough up is crucial, as well.

Makes:
about 10

Prep time:
15 minutes

Cook time:
15 minutes

These are amazing in the morning with a sausage gravy. My mom makes exceptional Oven "Fried" Chicken (page 58) and often serves it when we come over for Sunday dinner—everyone knows these light and flaky biscuits go hand-in-hand with fried chicken!

Flaky Sour Cream Biscuits

2 cups #1 All-Purpose Flour Blend (page 24)

2 tsp xanthan gum

2 tsp baking powder

1 tsp baking soda

1 tbsp pure cane sugar

½ tsp salt

5 tbsp Spectrum palm shortening

1 tsp apple cider vinegar

1 cup sour cream

1 large egg

1 tbsp water

1. Preheat the oven to 425°F (220°C) and line a baking sheet with parchment paper. In a medium bowl, whisk together the #1 All-Purpose Flour Blend, xanthan gum, baking powder, baking soda, sugar, and salt until combined.

2. Using a pastry cutter or fork, cut the shortening into the dry ingredients until pea-sized crumbs are formed.

3. In a small bowl, stir together the vinegar and sour cream. Using a wooden spoon, stir the mixture into the dry ingredients until just barely combined.

4. Turn the dough onto a cutting board lined with parchment paper. The dough will be very crumbly; squeeze the dough together until it holds the shape of a ball. It will have cracks in it. (If the dough becomes sticky, flour your hands.) In order to create flaky biscuits, do not overwork the dough.

5. Gently press the dough into a disk about 1-inch (2.5cm) thick. Cut out the biscuits using a biscuit cutter, about 2½-inches (6.25cm) in diameter. Continue gathering and shaping the scraps and cutting biscuits until you use all the dough.

6. In a small bowl, whisk together the egg and water. Brush the top of the biscuits with the egg wash.

7. Place the biscuits on the prepared baking sheet and bake for 15 minutes, or until lightly brown on top. Let cool on the pan for a few minutes. Serve warm with butter, honey, or jam.

Store it

Store in an airtight container on the counter for up to 2 days or in the freezer for up to 3 months. Thaw at room temperature.

Tip

If you need to use another brand of palm shortening, you may find your biscuits excessively spreading. Chill the dough for at least 1 hour before baking to help prevent the spreading.

Makes:
6–8

Prep time:
45 minutes, plus
45 minutes to rise

Cook time:
15 minutes

These are the closest thing to a donut-shop donut I have ever had. The creamy center helps create an incredibly light and moist donut. You do not need a deep fryer to make them—a frying pan works— although I do recommend the investment; it's worth it just for these!

Cream-Filled Donuts

3½ cups #2 All-Purpose Flour Blend (page 24), plus more to flour

2 tsp xanthan gum

¼ tsp salt

1 tbsp rapid-rise yeast

1¼ cups whole milk

2 large eggs, room temperature

1 tbsp apple cider vinegar

⅓ cup pure cane sugar, plus more to coat

½ cup salted butter, melted

High-heat oil (such as avocado oil), for frying

1 (5oz/140g) box Jell-O instant vanilla pudding, or Pastry Cream Filling (see page 165)

Store it

Store in an airtight container in the freezer for up to 3 months. Thaw at room temperature.

Tips

These are great as Boston Cream donuts. Just drizzle Chocolate Glaze (page 40) on top.

You can also make them jelly-filled by replacing the vanilla pudding with your favorite jelly or pie filling.

1. In a medium bowl, stir together the #2 All-Purpose Flour Blend, xanthan gum, salt, and yeast. Set aside.

2. On the stovetop over low heat or in the microwave, warm the milk to 105 to 110°F (40–43°C).

3. In a stand mixer fitted with the paddle attachment or in a large bowl, lightly beat the eggs on medium speed. To the eggs, add the warmed milk, vinegar, sugar, and butter, and beat on medium-low speed until combined.

4. Add the flour mixture to the milk mixture, and beat slowly on low speed to combine. Slowly increase the speed to medium and beat for 3 minutes more.

5. Turn the dough onto a well-floured surface. The dough will be very sticky and not as pliable as gluten-containing dough, so make sure you use plenty of flour.

6. Flour the top of the dough. Using a rolling pin, roll the dough out until ½-inch (1.25cm) thick. Use a round cookie or biscuit cutter to cut out the donuts. Continue gathering and shaping the scraps and cutting donuts until you use all the dough.

7. Transfer the donuts to a parchment-lined baking sheet and cover with another piece of parchment paper. Set in a warm place to rise for 30 to 45 minutes or until doubled in size.

8. While the donuts are rising, make the vanilla pudding according to the package directions. Set aside in the refrigerator until ready to use.

9. In a deep fryer or in a heavy-bottomed deep pot (with oil about 3-in/7.5cm deep), preheat the oil to 360°F (182°C). If the oil is too cold, the donuts will absorb too much oil and become heavy and greasy. If too hot, the donuts will brown too quickly and not be cooked enough in the middle. Fill a shallow dish with pure cane sugar for rolling the donuts in after frying.

10. Once the donuts have doubled in size and the oil is hot, carefully place one or two donuts at a time into the hot oil. Fry for 1 to 1½ minutes, and then flip. Fry for 1 minute more, and then remove. Let the donuts cool on a wire rack for just a minute or two, until cool enough to touch but still slightly hot. While the donuts are still warm, roll them in the sugar and then set on a wire rack to cool for 10 to 15 minutes. Repeat until all of the donuts are fried and coated.

11. Once the donuts have cooled, poke a hole on one side of each donut that goes to about the middle of the donut. (A chopstick works really well for this, or a thin sharp knife.) Fill a squeeze bottle or piping bag with the vanilla pudding. Squeeze the pudding into each donut until plump. These are best when served the same day.

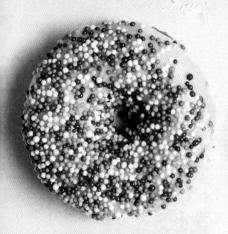

Vanilla Glaze:

4 tbsp salted butter, melted
1 tsp pure vanilla extract
1 tsp corn syrup
3 cups powdered sugar
⅓–½ cup whole milk
Sprinkles (optional), to decorate

In a medium bowl, stir the butter, vanilla, corn syrup, and powdered sugar until smooth. Add ⅓ cup milk and stir until smooth. Add more milk 1 tablespoon at a time until a thin icing forms. Dip the top of the cooled donuts in the glaze, and top with sprinkles (if using). Let rest on a wire rack until the glaze hardens.

Cinnamon-Sugar:

½ cup pure cane sugar
½ cup firmly packed light brown sugar
1 tbsp ground cinnamon
3 tbsp salted butter, melted

In a medium bowl, combine the cane sugar, brown sugar, and cinnamon. Brush the cooled donuts lightly with melted butter, and then roll them around in the cinnamon-sugar mixture until well coated.

Chocolate Glaze:

1½ cups powdered sugar
4 tbsp cocoa powder
3 tbsp whole milk
1 tsp pure vanilla extract
1 tsp corn syrup
Sprinkles (optional), to decorate

In a medium bowl, whisk together the powdered sugar and cocoa powder. Slowly stir in the milk, vanilla, and corn syrup, and whisk until smooth. Dip the top half of the cooled donuts in the glaze, and top with sprinkles (if using). Let rest on a wire rack until the glaze hardens.

Maple Glaze:

¼ cup salted butter
1 tsp corn syrup
⅓ cup pure maple syrup
1 cup powdered sugar

In a small saucepan over low heat, stir together the butter, corn syrup, and maple syrup. Once melted, remove from the heat and whisk in the powdered sugar. Let cool and thicken slightly. Dip the top half of the cooled donuts in the glaze. Let rest on a wire rack until the glaze hardens.

Powdered Sugar:

2 cups powdered sugar

Place the powdered sugar in a shallow dish. As soon as the donuts are cool enough to touch (but still very warm), roll them around in powdered sugar until well coated. Once cooled, re-roll them once or twice more.

Makes:
30 mini donuts
or 10 full-sized donuts

Prep time:
20 minutes, plus decorating

Cook time:
15 minutes

If asked "What's the first thing you'd eat if you could have gluten again?" hands down my response is "a DONUT!" I'm not sure I'll ever eat a donut-shop donut again, but these satisfy my cravings. Choose one variety, or make all five! This recipe is best in a donut maker, but if you're baking them, I recommend silicone molds.

Donuts 5 Ways

1 cup #1 All-Purpose Flour Blend (page 24)

1 tsp xanthan gum

¾ cup pure cane sugar

½ tsp baking soda

1 tsp baking powder

¼ tsp salt

1 large egg

½ cup whole milk

1 tsp apple cider vinegar

1 tsp pure vanilla extract

2 tbsp salted butter, melted

1. If using the oven instead of a donut maker, preheat the oven to 350°F (180°C). In a large bowl, whisk together the #1 All-Purpose Flour Blend, xanthan gum, sugar, baking soda, baking powder, and salt.

2. In a separate medium bowl, whisk the egg. Add the milk, vinegar, vanilla, and melted butter, and whisk until well combined.

3. Pour the wet ingredients into the dry ingredients and whisk until a thick, smooth batter forms. Let the batter sit for 5 to 10 minutes.

4. If using a donut maker, preheat and grease. If using donut pans in the oven, spray the pans with nonstick cooking spray.

5. Pour the batter into a piping bag or a resealable plastic bag. Cut the tip off of the icing bag or one corner of the plastic bag. Pipe the batter into the greased donut maker or donut pans, filling two-thirds full.

6. Bake in the donut maker for 3 to 5 minutes (or according to the manufacturer's instructions), or bake in the oven for 12 to 15 minutes or until golden brown.

7. Let cool on a wire rack (in the donut pans, if used) while preparing your desired toppings. If you are making powdered sugar donuts, roll them as soon as they're cool enough to touch.

Store it

Once completely cooled, store in an airtight container on the counter for 2 to 3 days or freeze for 2 to 3 months. Separate layers of donuts with parchment paper. Thaw in a single layer at room temperature.

Tips

The longer the batter sits, the fluffier the donuts will be. Prepare the batter up to 1 hour ahead of time.

Each topping recipe is enough for 1 batch. Plan your quantities accordingly if you'd like a variety of donuts.

These donuts can be very fun for every holiday by changing up the sprinkles you put on top—for example, orange and black for Halloween; or pink, red, and white for Valentine's day.

Fish & Poultry Mains

Macadamia Nut Crusted Halibut
with Mango Salsa 44

Tuna Noodle Casserole 46

Cracklin' Crab Cakes 47

California Seaside Fish 'n' Chips 49

Baja Fish Tacos 50

Chicken Shepherd's Pie 51

Pop's Chicken Wings with
Homemade Ranch Dressing 52

Chicken Parmesan 54

Divine Chicken Divan 55

World's Best Chicken Pot Pie 57

Oven "Fried" Chicken 58

Chicken Piccata 59

Chicken Salad 60

Creamy White Chicken Enchiladas 61

The light flavor and flakiness of halibut makes it my favorite fish, and the macadamia nut crust adds such a delicious twist. The mango salsa pairs just perfectly with this recipe. I try to always buy fresh halibut, but when it's not available, I purchase frozen skinless halibut, which works just as well.

Macadamia Nut Crusted Halibut
with Mango Salsa

½ cup #1 All-Purpose Flour Blend (page 24)

2 large eggs

¾ cup chopped, roasted, and salted macadamia nuts (processed until finely chopped)

1 tbsp chopped flat-leaf parsley

¼ tsp garlic powder

½ tsp salt

⅛ tsp freshly ground black pepper

2 tbsp unsweetened shredded coconut

¼ cup Homemade Breadcrumbs (page 25) or store-bought plain gluten-free breadcrumbs

4 halibut fillets (8oz/225g each)

Mango Salsa

1 cup chopped mango

3 tbsp chopped red onion

3 tbsp chopped cilantro

2 green onions, chopped

¼–½ jalapeño (to heat preference), finely diced

Juice of 1 lime

Salt and freshly ground black pepper, to taste

1. Preheat the oven to 400°F (200°C) and line a baking sheet with parchment paper. In a shallow bowl or on a large plate, add the #1 All-Purpose Flour Blend. In a second shallow bowl, beat the eggs. In a third shallow bowl or on a large plate, stir together the macadamia nuts, parsley, garlic powder, salt, pepper, coconut, and Homemade Breadcrumbs.

2. Dredge the fish fillets in the #1 All-Purpose Flour Blend, shaking off any excess. Then dip into the beaten eggs. Finally coat in the nut mixture, pressing the fish firmly into the nut mixture to coat all sides thoroughly. Carefully place the fillets onto the prepared baking sheet.

3. Bake for 20 to 25 minutes or until golden brown, no longer opaque in the center, and flakes easily. If the macadamia crust starts to get too brown, cover with a piece of parchment paper. Serve immediately with the mango salsa on top.

Mango Salsa: You can prepare this while the fish is cooking. In a small bowl, stir together the mango, red onion, cilantro, green onions, jalapeño, lime juice, salt, and pepper. Refrigerate until ready to use.

I grew up on comforting casserole dishes, and tuna noodle casserole was always one of my favorites. My husband says that even if this was the only recipe in the whole book, it would still sell. It's very easy to customize this dish by mixing up the vegetables or any other additional ingredients you'd like to add.

Tuna Noodle Casserole

1¼ cups uncooked gluten-free pasta shells or elbows (such as Tinkyada)

4 tbsp salted butter, divided

1 celery stalk, finely chopped

¼ cup finely chopped yellow onion

2 tbsp #1 All-Purpose Flour Blend (page 24)

½ tsp salt

¼ tsp freshly ground black pepper

2 cups whole milk

2 cups shredded sharp Cheddar cheese, divided

1 cup frozen peas

2 (5oz/140g) cans tuna in water, drained

½ cup Homemade Breadcrumbs (page 25) or store-bought plain gluten-free breadcrumbs

1. Preheat the oven to 350°F (180°C). Bring a medium pot of salted water to a boil, and add the pasta. Cook the pasta for 3 to 5 minutes less than the package instructions. Drain the pasta and immediately rinse under cold water.

2. In a large saucepan, melt 2 tablespoons butter over medium heat. Add the celery and onion and sauté until soft and translucent.

3. Add 1 tablespoon more butter to the saucepan, and stir until melted. Stir in the #1 All-Purpose Flour Blend, salt, and pepper. Stir constantly over medium heat until smooth and bubbly.

4. Gradually stir in the milk and bring to a boil, constantly stirring. Once the milk begins to boil, stir for 1 minute more.

5. Stir in 1½ cups Cheddar until melted, and then remove from the heat. Fold in the pasta, frozen peas, and tuna until well mixed.

6. Pour into a 2-quart (2 liter) casserole dish and sprinkle the remaining ½ cup Cheddar on top. Cover and cook for 25 minutes or until bubbly.

7. While casserole is cooking, prepare the crumb topping. In a small bowl, melt the remaining 1 tablespoon butter. Stir in the Homemade Breadcrumbs.

8. After 25 minutes, uncover the casserole. Sprinkle the breadcrumb topping on top and cook, uncovered, for an additional 5 minutes. Let rest for 5 minutes and serve.

Makes:
10

Prep time:
15 minutes

Cook time:
20 minutes

These crab cakes are prepared with gluten-free crackers and real crabmeat (imitation crabmeat contains wheat), and then baked instead of fried. They are moist on the inside and crispy on the outside without any of the frying oil. Serve alongside homemade cocktail sauce and a lemon slice for a great appetizer or main dish.

Cracklin' Crab Cakes

1 large egg
½ tsp salt
¼ tsp freshly ground
    black pepper
¼ tsp celery salt
¼ tsp paprika
3 tbsp mayonnaise
1 tsp fresh lemon juice
1 tbsp Dijon mustard
1 tsp Worcestershire sauce
    (gluten-free)
1 tbsp chopped chives
1 tbsp chopped flat-leaf parsley
1 lb (450g) fresh real crabmeat
    (thawed, moisture squeezed
    out, and patted dry if frozen)
1 cup crushed gluten-free
    saltine-style crackers
    (see the tip)
Cooking spray, to coat

Cocktail Sauce

¼ cup ketchup
2 tsp prepared horseradish
    (gluten-free)
¼ tsp fresh lemon juice
½ tsp light brown sugar

1. Preheat the oven to 400°F (200°C) and line a baking sheet with parchment paper.

2. In a large bowl, whisk the egg. Add the salt, pepper, celery salt, paprika, mayonnaise, lemon juice, Dijon, Worcestershire sauce, chives, and parsley. Whisk until well combined.

3. Stir in the crabmeat until well combined. Gently stir in the crushed crackers until well combined.

4. Using a ⅓ cup measuring cup, scoop out the crab mixture and use your hands to form into patties. Be sure to squeeze the mixture tightly so the cakes will not fall apart when baked. Place the cakes on the prepared baking sheet.

5. Lightly spray each cake with cooking spray and bake for 7 minutes. Flip the cakes, spray with cooking spray, and bake for an additional 7 minutes.

6. Turn the oven to broil and broil both sides of the cakes for a couple minutes to crisp up the outside. Serve immediately with lemon wedges and homemade cocktail sauce.

Cocktail Sauce: In a small bowl, stir together the ketchup, horseradish, lemon juice, and brown sugar until well combined. Refrigerate until ready to use.

Store it

Wrap each crab cake individually in plastic wrap. Store in an airtight container in the freezer for up to 3 months.

Tip

My favorite cracker brand is Schar, however you can use any gluten-free cracker that resembles a saltine. You may also substitute breadcrumbs. To crush, place the whole crackers in a resealable bag, seal, and roll a rolling pin over it until finely crushed.

Tip

The secret to this light and tender gluten-free coating is the soda. (Many fish 'n' chip recipes use beer in the batter.) The carbonation creates little air pockets, which provide lift.

Serves:
4

Prep time:
1½ hours, plus
1 hour to soak

Cook time:
20 minutes

Gluten-free fried foods are almost impossible to find when you are eating out. Living in Southern California, fish 'n' chips are on menus at restaurants all over town and they always smell so good! These gluten-free fish 'n' chips will rival any you would get in a restaurant.

California Seaside Fish 'n' Chips

3 large russet potatoes, peeled and sliced into ¼-in (0.5cm) thick strips

High-heat oil (such as avocado oil), for frying (6–12 cups)

1½ cups #1 All-Purpose Flour Blend (page 24), divided

1 tsp garlic salt

1 tsp lemon pepper seasoning

3 large egg whites

1½ tsp baking powder

½ tsp xanthan gum

1½ tsp salt, plus more to season

1½–2½ cups lemon-lime soda (such as Sprite or 7-Up)

1½lb (680g) skinless cod, haddock, or halibut fillets

Tartar Sauce

¼ cup mayonnaise

1½ tbsp sweet pickle relish

½ tsp dried parsley

1 tsp finely grated onion

Salt and freshly ground black pepper, to taste

1. Soak the potato strips in cold water for at least 1 hour, or up to 24 hours. Drain, rinse well, and spread out the strips on paper towels to dry.

2. Once dry, pre-fry the potatoes. Fill a deep fryer, heavy-bottomed deep pot, or Dutch oven with oil about 3 inches (7.5cm) high. Heat the oil to 325°F (170°C). (This specific temperature is important; if the oil is not hot enough, the food will absorb too much oil and become dense and soggy.)

3. Working in batches so you don't overcrowd the pot, carefully add the potato strips to the hot oil. Fry for 3 minutes, drain, and spread out on a paper towel–lined baking sheet. (The potatoes will not be fully cooked at this point, but you will fry them again later.)

4. Prepare three shallow dishes. In the first, stir together ½ cup #1 All-Purpose Flour Blend, garlic salt, and lemon pepper seasoning. In the second, whisk the egg whites. In the third, whisk together the remaining 1 cup #1 All-Purpose Flour Blend, baking powder, xanthan gum, and salt. Gradually whisk in the lemon-lime soda until smooth—the batter should be the consistency of runny pancake batter; if it's too thick, gradually whisk in more soda 1 tablespoon at a time to reach the desired consistency, and if it's too thin, whisk in more flour 1 tablespoon at a time.

5. Increase the oil temperature to 375°F (190°C). Dredge the fish in the dry flour mixture, then in the egg whites, allowing any extra to drip off, and then dip the fish in the wet batter, allowing excess to fall off.

6. Working in batches to avoid overcrowding, place the fish and a handful of pre-fried potatoes in the oil and cook until golden brown, 5 to 7 minutes.

7. Strain the fish and fried potatoes and transfer to a paper towel–lined baking sheet or cooling rack. Sprinkle salt on the fries. Continue frying the rest of the fish and chips. Serve immediately with tartar sauce.

Tartar Sauce: In a small bowl, stir together the mayonnaise, relish, parsley, onion, salt, and pepper. Refrigerate until ready to serve.

Air Fryer Method: Prepare the fries in an air fryer for perfect crispiness. (You cannot use the air fryer to cook the fish—the batter is too runny.) Preheat the fryer to 400°F (200°C). No need to soak or pre-fry the potatoes. Working in batches so you don't overcrowd the fryer basket, cook for 20 to 25 minutes, shaking the basket every 5 to 8 minutes so they brown evenly.

We love to prepare this easy recipe for midweek meals. The white sauce mixed with the pico de gallo is what makes it so spectacular! I will often pour the two on top of beans and rice the next day for leftovers. You could substitute chicken for the fish if preferred, and it will taste just as amazing!

Baja Fish Tacos

6 (4–6oz/110–170g) fish fillets (halibut or any mild white fish)

Lemon pepper seasoning, to taste

Garlic salt, to taste

½ head green cabbage

8–10 corn tortillas

Cooked rice, to serve

Pico de Gallo

5–6 Roma tomatoes, diced

3 tbsp chopped red onion

1 clove garlic, minced

1 tsp garlic salt

2 heaping tbsp chopped cilantro (stems and leaves)

Freshly ground black pepper, to taste

White Sauce

½ cup mayonnaise

2 tbsp whole milk

1 tsp fresh lemon juice

½ tsp garlic salt

Pinch of chipotle pepper (optional)

Black Beans

1 tbsp avocado oil

¼ cup chopped onion

2 cloves garlic, minced

1 (15oz/420g) can black beans

⅛ tsp chili powder

¼ tsp ground cumin

¼ tsp dried oregano

½ tsp garlic salt

1. Preheat the grill (see the tip) or preheat a grill pan on the stove over medium-high heat. Season the fish with lemon pepper seasoning and garlic salt. Cook the fish for 5 to 7 minutes per side or until no longer opaque in the center and it flakes easily with a fork.

2. While the fish is cooking, shred the cabbage and warm the tortillas on the stove.

3. Assemble the tacos. Layer the fish, cabbage, pico de gallo, and white sauce in the corn tortillas, and serve alongside black beans and rice.

Pico de Gallo: In a small bowl, stir together the tomatoes, red onion, garlic, garlic salt, cilantro, and pepper. Adjust the seasonings to taste and refrigerate until ready to use.

White Sauce: In a small bowl, whisk together the mayonnaise, milk, lemon juice, garlic salt, and chipotle pepper, and refrigerate until ready to use.

Black Beans: In a medium pot, heat the avocado oil. Sauté the onions until tender and translucent, about 5 minutes. Add the garlic and cook for 1 minute. Stir in the black beans, chili powder, cumin, oregano, and garlic salt, and bring to a boil. Reduce to a simmer for 5 to 10 minutes. Then in a blender, process ¼ cup beans with the juices until smooth. Mix back in with the beans and keep warm until ready to serve.

Tips

Make the pico de gallo and white sauce in the morning. The longer the two sit and marinate, the more flavorful they will be. Plus, dinner prep will be that much easier.

We prefer the flavor of grilling the fish; however, fillets can be tricky on the grill because they often fall apart, stick, or fall through the grate. For the best success, you can either brush the grates with olive oil before placing the fish on the grill, or grease a piece of aluminum foil and use it as a pan on the grill.

I grew up on this chicken shepherd's pie and had no idea until I was older that shepherd's pie is usually made with ground lamb and a brown gravy sauce. To this day, I still have never tried a traditional Irish shepherd's pie, and once you try this one, you might never feel the need to go back, either! This recipe is full of comforting flavor.

Chicken Shepherd's Pie

Mashed Potatoes

1½ tsp salt, divided

3lb (1.5kg) russet potatoes, peeled and cubed

5 tbsp salted butter

¼ tsp freshly ground black pepper

¼ cup sour cream (optional; for extra creaminess)

Filling

2½–3 cups uncooked chicken cubes (1-in/2.5cm pieces)

½ cup chopped yellow onion

½ cup chopped celery

2 cloves garlic, minced

1 tsp salt

½ tsp freshly ground black pepper

1½–2 cups chicken stock

1 cup carrot slices (¼-in/0.5cm pieces)

1 tsp dried thyme

1 tsp dried parsley

⅓ cup plus 2 tbsp #1 All-Purpose Flour Blend (page 24)

½ cup frozen peas

1½ cups shredded Cheddar cheese

1. Prepare the mashed potatoes. Bring a large pot of water with 1 teaspoon salt to a boil. Add the potato cubes and cook for 18 to 20 minutes or until fork-tender.

2. Reserve 1¼ cups cooking water, and then drain the potatoes. Place the potatoes in the bowl of a stand mixer or in a large bowl. Use a potato masher to mash the potatoes.

3. Slowly beat the potatoes on low speed while adding ½ cup of the reserved cooking liquid. Add the butter, the remaining ½ tsp salt, pepper, and sour cream (if using). Slowly increase the speed to medium-high, and beat until smooth and fluffy, 1 to 2 minutes. If too thick, add more reserved cooking liquid until you reach the desired consistency. Set aside.

4. Prepare the filling. Preheat the oven to 350°F (180°C). In a medium saucepan, evenly arrange the cubed chicken. Add the onion, celery, garlic, salt, and pepper.

5. Pour in enough chicken stock to just cover the chicken and vegetables (about 1½ cups). Bring to a boil, cover, and reduce the heat to low. Cook for 15 minutes.

6. Uncover the chicken, turn the heat to medium-high, and add the carrots, thyme, and parsley. Cook for 5 minutes.

7. In a small bowl, whisk the #1 All-Purpose Flour Blend with ¼ cup chicken stock. Stir into the chicken mixture, along with the peas. Cook until thick and bubbly.

8. Pour the mixture into a 2½-quart (2.5 liter) baking dish. If the potatoes have become too thick from sitting, add the reserved cooking liquid 1 tablespoon at a time until smooth and easy to spread. Gently spread the mashed potatoes evenly over the chicken mixture.

9. Sprinkle the Cheddar on top of the mashed potatoes. Bake for 25 to 30 minutes or until heated through and bubbling. Let sit for 5 minutes before serving.

Tips

If the filling is too runny, the mashed potatoes will have a hard time "sitting" on top and will sink into the filling mixture. To prevent this, avoid using too much chicken stock when cooking the chicken; use just enough to barely cover the chicken and no more than 2 cups total in the whole recipe. If the filling still seems too watery toward the end of cooking, you can add more flour to the filling mixture, 1 tablespoon at a time, until thick and bubbly.

There is nothing better than a plate of hot chicken wings and ranch dressing when watching a football game. My dad has been making these wings for every sporting event on TV for years. They are so easy, have just the right amount of heat, and are sure to satisfy your guests. But have wet wipes ready—they are messy!

Pop's Chicken Wings
with Homemade Ranch Dressing

1 tsp garlic powder

1 tsp onion powder

1 tsp salt

½ tsp paprika

½ tsp freshly ground
   black pepper

3–4lb (1.5–2kg) split chicken
   wings

1 cup salted butter (or less if
   you prefer a hotter sauce)

1 (12oz/340g) jar hot sauce
   (such as Frank's)

Ranch Dressing

½ cup mayonnaise

½ cup sour cream

½ cup buttermilk

1½ tsp fresh lemon juice

½ tsp garlic powder

2 tbsp chopped chives

3 tbsp chopped flat-leaf parsley

½ tsp dried dill

½ tsp onion powder

½ tsp salt

¼ tsp freshly ground
   black pepper

1. Preheat the oven to 425°F (220°C). Prepare the chicken wings. In a small bowl, stir together the garlic powder, onion powder, salt, paprika, and pepper.

2. In a large bowl, toss the spice blend with the chicken wings until the wings are evenly coated.

3. Grease the bottom of a large rimmed baking sheet or 9 x 13-inch (23 x 33cm) baking dish. Spread the wings out on the prepared pan and bake for 30 to 40 minutes or until browned.

4. Meanwhile, in a small bowl, whisk together the melted butter and hot sauce. Remove the wings from the oven. In a large bowl, toss the wings with the hot sauce mixture.

5. Turn the oven to broil. Spread the wings back out onto the baking pan and broil for 1 to 2 minutes or until crispy.

6. Arrange the wings on a platter. Serve hot with any remaining hot sauce from the large bowl and ranch dressing for dipping.

Ranch Dressing: In a small bowl, stir together all of the ingredients and refrigerate until ready to serve. Prepare this up to 2 days ahead of time so the flavors can meld.

Air Fryer Method: An air fryer gets these wings extra crispy in a way the oven cannot. Prepare the wings as described in steps 1 and 2. Working in batches as needed, place the wings in the air fryer basket (do not overcrowd; wings shouldn't be touching) and spray all sides of the wings with cooking spray. Set the air fryer to 375°F (190°C), and cook for 25 minutes, shaking the basket halfway through cooking. Then increase the temperature to 400°F (200°C) and cook for an additional 5 minutes. Remove from the air fryer and toss immediately in the hot sauce mixture.

We enjoy eating this Chicken Parmesan alongside steamed broccoli, but it is also very good served on top of gluten-free spaghetti. The homemade Mom's Famous Meat Sauce is what makes this dish so special, but you can substitute any meat sauce.

Chicken Parmesan

3 large boneless, skinless chicken breasts, butterflied

½ cup #1 All-Purpose Flour Blend (page 24)

1 tsp garlic salt

2 large eggs

1 cup Homemade Breadcrumbs (page 25) or store-bought plain gluten-free breadcrumbs

1 tsp dried basil

1 tsp dried oregano

1 tsp dried parsley

½ tsp salt

¼ tsp freshly ground black pepper

2 tbsp avocado oil

4–5 cups Mom's Famous Meat Sauce (page 82) or your favorite meat sauce

Grated Parmesan cheese, to top

12oz (340g) block mozzarella cheese, cut into 12 slices

1. Preheat the oven to 375°F (190°C) and lightly grease the bottom of a large rimmed baking sheet with cooking spray.

2. One at a time, place the butterflied chicken breasts between two sheets of parchment paper or plastic wrap and pound out until about ¼-inch (0.5cm) thick.

3. Prepare three shallow dishes. In the first, stir together the #1 All-Purpose Flour Blend and garlic salt. In the second, beat the eggs. In the third, stir together the Homemade Breadcrumbs, basil, oregano, parsley, salt, and pepper.

4. In a large skillet, heat the avocado oil over medium-high heat. Dredge each chicken breast in the #1 All-Purpose Flour Blend, then in the eggs, letting any excess drip off, and then coat thoroughly in the breadcrumb mixture.

5. Fry for 3 to 4 minutes on each side or until golden brown. Add more oil if the pan becomes too dry. Transfer the chicken breasts to the baking sheet.

6. Top each piece of chicken with ¼ to ⅓ cup Mom's Famous Meat Sauce, sprinkle with Parmesan, and then cover each piece of chicken with 2 slices mozzarella.

7. Bake for 20 minutes, or until the sauce is bubbly and the cheese is melted and golden brown. Serve immediately.

Serves:
6

Prep time:
15 minutes

Cook time:
40 minutes

Any time I ask my husband what he wants for dinner, the answer is chicken divan, his all-time favorite dish. He loves anything with sauce, and this recipe, using only three ingredients, creates a creamy, flavorful sauce that the broccoli and chicken soak right up.

Divine Chicken Divan

1½lb (680g) broccoli florets, cut into bite-sized pieces (3 very large florets)

3 cups cooked cubed chicken breasts or rotisserie chicken

2 (12oz/340g) boxes condensed gluten-free cream of chicken soup (such as Pacific)

1 cup mayonnaise

1 tsp fresh lemon juice

4oz (110g) Cheddar cheese, shredded (about 1 cup)

1. Preheat the oven to 350°F (180°C). Add the broccoli florets to a large pot, and cover with about 2 inches (5cm) water. Cover and cook over high heat for 4 to 6 minutes depending on the desired tenderness.

2. Drain the broccoli and spread out evenly in a 9 x 13-inch (23 x 33cm) baking dish. Arrange the cooked chicken cubes evenly over the broccoli.

3. In a medium bowl, stir together the soup, mayonnaise, and lemon juice until well combined. Pour the soup mixture on top of the chicken and broccoli and spread out evenly. Be sure to cover every piece of chicken and broccoli so that they do not dry out when cooking.

4. Sprinkle the Cheddar evenly over the top of the casserole. Bake for 30 to 35 minutes or until bubbly. Let rest for 5 to 10 minutes before serving.

Tip

You can prep this meal up to 24 hours ahead of baking. Cover the fully prepared casserole and refrigerate until ready to bake.

Makes:
1 (9-in/23cm) pie
or 8–10 mini pies

Prep time:
40 minutes

Cook time:
55 minutes

I have been told, "This is the best chicken pot pie I have ever had!" It has a flaky, buttery crust, and a rich, creamy filling of chicken and vegetables. I love to make these as individual servings so everyone can have their own pie, or you can stock the freezer and have them ready for lunches and dinners.

World's Best Chicken Pot Pie

2 unbaked Buttery Pie Crusts (page 138)

1 cup peeled and diced russet potatoes

¾ cup sliced carrots

2½ tsp salt, divided

½ cup salted butter

⅓ cup chopped yellow onion

⅓ cup chopped celery

2 cloves garlic, minced

¼ tsp freshly ground black pepper

¼ tsp garlic powder

¼ tsp onion powder

½ cup #1 All-Purpose Flour Blend (page 24)

1½ cups chicken stock

½ cup dry white wine (or ¼ cup white wine vinegar plus ¼ cup water)

¾ cup whole milk

2 cups cooked cubed chicken (such as rotisserie chicken)

½ cup frozen peas

1½ tsp dried parsley

1 tsp dried thyme

1 large egg

1. Mold one pie crust into a 9-inch (23cm) deep-dish pie pan and freeze until ready to use. Refrigerate the other rolled-out pie crust, pulling it out of the refrigerator 5 minutes before you'll need it. Preheat the oven to 425°F (220°C).

2. In a small saucepan, add the potatoes, carrots, and ½ tsp salt. Add water to just cover the vegetables. Bring to a boil over high heat. Reduce the heat to low, cover, and cook for 8 minutes. Strain and set aside.

3. In a large skillet, heat the butter over medium-high heat. Add the onions and celery and sauté until tender. Add the garlic and cook for 1 minute more. Add the pepper, 1½ tsp salt, garlic powder, onion powder, and #1 All-Purpose Flour Blend, and stir until combined. Gradually stir in the stock, wine, and milk. Cook, stirring constantly, until thick and bubbly.

4. Stir in the chicken, peas, parsley, thyme, and potato mixture. Taste and adjust the seasoning as desired. Remove from the heat.

5. Remove the pie crust from the freezer and fill with the chicken mixture. Place the top crust over the filling and seal the edges.

6. In a small bowl, whisk together the egg and 1 tablespoon water. Brush the top of the pie with the egg wash, and then cut 1 or 2 slits in the top crust.

7. Bake for 35 to 40 minutes or until the crust is lightly browned. Check the pie halfway through cooking; if the edges are getting too brown, cover them with foil. Let rest for 15 minutes before serving.

Mini Pies: Using two Buttery Pie Crusts and 4-inch (10cm) pans, this recipe will make 8 to 10 mini pies. (You will not place a bottom crust into the tins.)

In step 1, cut the rolled-out pie crusts into circles to fit on top of your pies; then refrigerate. (You don't need to freeze any crust). In step 5, fill each pan almost to the top with the filling; be sure to seal the top crust to your pans so the filling does not bubble out.

This chicken contains all the flavor and crispiness of fried chicken without actually being fried. The high heat of the oven gets the skin nice and crispy, and the gluten-free flour coating is full of spices and flavor. My whole family loves fried chicken, and this is just like a bucket from KFC.

Oven "Fried" Chicken

3–3½lb (1.5kg–1.6kg) chicken thighs and drumsticks, bone-in and skin-on, trimmed of any excess skin

2 cups buttermilk

2¼ cups #1 All-Purpose Flour Blend (page 24)

¾ tsp xanthan gum

3 tsp paprika

3 tsp salt

¾ tsp freshly ground black pepper

¾ tsp garlic powder

¾ tsp onion powder

⅓ cup freshly grated Parmesan cheese

½ cup salted butter

1. Divide the chicken pieces evenly between two resealable plastic bags. Add 1 cup buttermilk to each bag. Place in the refrigerator, making sure all chicken pieces are coated. Marinate all day or overnight.

2. Preheat the oven to 425°F (220°C). In a small bowl, stir together the #1 All-Purpose Flour Blend, xanthan gum, paprika, salt, pepper, garlic powder, onion powder, and Parmesan until well combined.

3. Pour the flour mixture into a separate gallon-sized resealable bag. One piece at a time, add the chicken pieces to the bag, seal, and shake until well coated. Place the coated chicken pieces on a wire rack. Repeat until all pieces have been coated. Repeat with all of the chicken pieces for a second coat. Discard the buttermilk.

4. Place the butter in a large rimmed baking sheet and melt in the oven. Once the butter has melted, place the chicken skin side down in the pan and bake for 40 minutes.

5. Very carefully so you don't lose any of the coating, flip the chicken with a spatula and fork (see the tip) and bake for an additional 20 to 30 minutes or until the internal temperature reaches 165°F (75°C) and the skin is very crispy. Serve immediately.

Air Fryer Method: Follow the instructions through step 3. Preheat the air fryer to 350°F (180°C). Spray the skin side of the chicken with cooking oil. Place the chicken pieces skin side down into the air fryer basket. Spray the other side with cooking oil. Air fry for 15 minutes. Flip the chicken and spray with more cooking oil if the skin is looking dry or any flour has not been coated with oil. Cook for an additional 10 to 12 minutes or until the internal temperature reaches 165°F (75°C).

Tips

The coating falls off very easily when flipping the chicken. Use a spatula to scrape under the chicken when flipping, and use a fork to help gently guide it onto its other side. Using tongs is a little too rough and will scrape the coating off. A fish spatula also works.

Chicken piccata always seems like a fancy dish you can order only in restaurants, but it is actually very easy to make using very few ingredients. Serve this dish to your family, and they will think they just sat down at an elegant Italian restaurant.

Chicken Piccata

1½lb (680kg) thin-cut chicken breast cutlets or butterflied boneless, skinless chicken breasts

1 cup #1 All-Purpose Flour Blend (page 24)

½ tsp garlic salt

¼ tsp freshly ground black pepper, plus more to season

4 tbsp freshly grated Parmesan cheese

2 tbsp avocado oil

4 tbsp salted butter, divided

Salt, to season

¼ cup chicken stock

⅓ cup white wine

3 tbsp fresh lemon juice

¼ cup capers in brine

1½ tsp chopped flat-leaf parsley

1. Preheat a small dish in the oven at 275°F (140°C) to keep the cooked chicken warm. One at a time, place the chicken between two sheets of parchment paper or plastic wrap and pound out until about ¼-inch (0.5cm) thick.

2. In a shallow dish, stir together the #1 All-Purpose Flour Blend, garlic salt, pepper, and Parmesan.

3. In a large skillet, heat the avocado oil over medium-high heat. Melt 2 tablespoons butter in the oil.

4. Salt and pepper both sides of each chicken breast, and then dredge each piece in the flour mixture. Fry each piece of flour-coated chicken in the butter and oil for 4 to 5 minutes per side, or until cooked all the way through and golden brown. Transfer each piece of cooked chicken to the dish in the oven until needed.

5. In the same pan used to fry the chicken, add the chicken stock, wine, lemon juice, and capers, and deglaze the pan. Lower the heat to medium and reduce the liquid by half.

6. Whisk in the remaining 2 tablespoons butter and the parsley. Stir until the butter is melted. Return the chicken to the pan over medium heat and slightly reduce the sauce. Serve immediately.

Tip

Prepare some of this dish ahead of time. Pound the chicken up to 1 day in advance, storing it in the refrigerator separated by pieces of parchment paper in a resealable bag. You can also mix together the flour, seasonings, and Parmesan and store in the refrigerator until ready to use.

Serves:
3–4

Prep time:
15 minutes, plus
30 minutes to chill

Cook time:
None

The dill pickles give this chicken salad a bit of sour flavor that is perfectly balanced by the sweetness in the carrots. I started putting the carrots in this salad for a little additional nutrition, and we loved the flavor so much that now it's a standard ingredient.

Chicken Salad

½ cup mayonnaise
1 tsp Dijon mustard
¼ tsp dried dill
1 tbsp finely diced red onion
2 tbsp finely diced celery
2–3 tbsp finely diced dill pickle
2 cups diced cooked chicken
   (such as rotisserie)
1 small carrot, grated
Salt and freshly ground black
   pepper, to taste
Easy White Sandwich Bread
   (page 113) or store-bought
   gluten-free bread; lettuce; or
   gluten-free crackers and
   celery sticks, to serve

1. In a medium bowl, stir together the mayonnaise, mustard, dill, onion, and celery.

2. Gently stir in the pickles and chicken. Fold in the grated carrot and season with salt and pepper to taste.

3. Chill for at least 30 minutes. Serve on slices of bread, atop a bed of lettuce, or with crackers and celery sticks for scooping.

Tips

This chicken salad works great as a party appetizer. You can serve it in a bowl with crackers or carrot and celery sticks to use for dipping. You can also put small amounts into bite-sized pieces of radicchio lettuce.

These white chicken enchiladas are smothered in a simple, rich, creamy sauce and topped with cheese. I can honestly say this was my favorite meal growing up, and with a great gluten-free flour tortilla, this is pretty close to the recipe of my memories.

Creamy White Chicken Enchiladas

1 (12oz/340g) box condensed gluten-free cream of chicken soup (such as Pacific)

½ yellow onion, chopped

1 (3.5oz/100g) can diced green chiles

1 cup sour cream

½lb (225g) Monterey Jack cheese, shredded, divided

2½ cups cooked cubed or shredded chicken (such as rotisserie)

8 Flour Tortillas (page 117) or store-bought gluten-free flour tortillas (such as Mission)

1. Preheat the oven to 350°F (180°C) and lightly grease the bottom of a 9 x 13-inch (23 x 33cm) casserole dish. In a medium bowl, mix the cream of chicken soup, onions, chiles, sour cream, and half of the Monterey Jack.

2. In a separate large bowl, stir together the chicken with half of the sauce.

3. Place one-eighth of the chicken mixture on each tortilla, roll, and arrange seam side down in the prepared pan.

4. Pour the remaining cream sauce over the enchiladas, and spread out evenly. Sprinkle the remaining Monterey Jack on top of the enchiladas.

5. Bake for 30 to 40 minutes or until hot and bubbly. Let rest for 5 to 10 minutes before serving.

Tip ....

Serve with sour cream and your favorite salsa or hot sauce. Salsa verde is excellent with these enchiladas.

Pork & Beef Mains

Pork Chops with Mushroom Gravy......64

Heavenly Dijon Pork Chops................66

Easy Crockpot Salsa Verde Pork.........67

Papa Motte's Pork Fried Rice............69

Linda's Luscious Pork Tenderloin.......70

Classic Beef Stroganoff.......................71

Steak Sandwiches with
    Horseradish Cream Sauce..................72

Papa's Meaty Chili.............................74

Grandma Joy's Swiss Steak.................75

Mama's Enchilada Pie.......................77

Chinese Takeout Beef & Broccoli
    Stir-Fry.......................................78

Meaty Lasagna.................................79

Homemade Meatballs.........................80

Mom's Famous Meat Sauce.................82

Meatloaf with Balsamic Glaze............83

My family has dinner at my mom and dad's house almost every Sunday, and this dish is a staple. As I've mentioned, my family loves anything with sauce on it! Plus, with five grandsons who love to eat, this is one we can easily make in bulk. Serve with mashed potatoes, rice, noodles, asparagus, or green beans.

Pork Chops
with Mushroom Gravy

3 tbsp salted butter, divided

10–12 thin-cut boneless pork chops (or 5–6 thick boneless pork chops, butterflied)

Salt and freshly ground black pepper, to taste

1 small yellow onion, halved and thinly sliced

8oz (225g) sliced mushrooms

2 (12oz/340g) boxes condensed gluten-free cream of mushroom soup (such as Pacific)

1. In a large deep skillet or an electric skillet, melt 2 tablespoons butter over medium-high heat.

2. Season both sides of the pork chops with salt and pepper. Brown in the melted butter for 2 to 3 minutes per side. Remove the pork chops and set aside.

3. Melt the remaining 1 tablespoon butter in the skillet and add the onion slices and mushrooms. Cook for 6 to 8 minutes or until tender. Stir in the boxes of cream of mushroom soup.

4. Add the pork chops back to the skillet. Bring to a simmer, reduce the heat to low, cover, and cook for 45 to 60 minutes, stirring occasionally, until the pork chops are tender. Serve immediately.

Tip
Slowly cooking these chops over very low heat is what makes them so tender. Don't rush the process!

Serves:
6

Prep time:
10 minutes

Cook time:
45 minutes

Pork chops can be tricky and often turn out dry because they are a relatively quick-cooking lean meat. However, with the chops slowly cooked over low heat and smothered in this light and creamy sauce, there is nothing dry about them! This recipe is great served alongside white rice and with roasted or grilled asparagus.

Heavenly Dijon Pork Chops

1 tbsp salted butter

1 tbsp avocado oil

6 pork chops (boneless or bone-in)

Salt and freshly ground black pepper, to taste

¼ cup chopped shallots

½ cup dry white wine

¾ cup chicken stock

1 tbsp #1 All-Purpose Flour Blend (page 24)

½ cup heavy whipping cream

2 tsp Dijon mustard

1 tbsp chopped flat-leaf parsley

1. In a large deep skillet, melt the butter and the oil over medium-high heat. Season the pork chops with salt and pepper on both sides. Brown for 2 to 3 minutes per side.

2. Remove the chops to a plate and pour off all but 1 tablespoon fat from the pan. Add the shallots and cook until softened, about 2 minutes.

3. Add the wine, deglaze the pan, and bring to a boil. Stir in the stock and return the pork chops to the pan.

4. Bring the sauce to a simmer, lower the heat to medium-low, cover, and cook until the pork chops are tender, about 20 minutes. Remove the pork chops to a serving dish. Cover to keep warm.

5. Raise the heat to medium-high and boil the juices in the pan until reduced by half. Whisk in the #1 All-Purpose Flour Blend. Whisk in the cream and mustard and boil for 2 more minutes, or until the sauce has thickened. Stir in the parsley and remove from the heat.

6. Taste the sauce and season with salt and pepper. Pour the sauce over the pork chops and serve immediately.

If you're in need of a super easy no-prep meal, then here you go! With only two ingredients, it has as much flavor as if you had spent all day cutting, chopping, and cooking. It's also very versatile—use it for taco meat with shredded lettuce, sour cream, chopped onions, cilantro, and shredded cheese, or serve it over rice with black beans.

Easy Crockpot Salsa Verde Pork

3–4lb (1.5–2kg) boneless pork roast
1–2 (16oz/450g) jars salsa verde (such as Frontera)

1. Cut the pork roast into 3 or 4 large chunks and place the pork in a slow cooker. Add in 1 to 2 jars of salsa verde. The more salsa you use, the saucier the pork will be in the end. One jar mostly just flavors the pork, while two jars create a verde sauce for the pork to soak in.

2. Cook on low for 8 hours. After the cooking is complete, shred the pork with two forks. Stir until the meat is well combined with the salsa and juices. Serve immediately.

Store it

Store in an airtight container in the freezer for up to 3 months. Thaw in the refrigerator overnight or slowly reheat in a pot on the stovetop.

Tip

If you want a little more flavor, season the pork with salt and freshly ground black pepper and brown in oil for 5 to 10 minutes before throwing into the slow cooker.

Serves:
4 for dinner or
6–8 as a side

Prep time:
15 minutes

Cook time:
25 minutes

My dad often makes a large batch of this rice, and he and my mom will have it for lunch or will snack on it all week. Chinese food has always been one of my favorites, but I have never found a Chinese restaurant that serves gluten-free food. This fried rice uses tamari (a gluten-free soy sauce) or coconut aminos, making it wheat-free.

Papa Motte's Pork Fried Rice

3 thin-cut boneless pork chops

½ tsp salt

¼ tsp freshly ground black pepper

3 tbsp avocado oil, divided

½ tsp toasted sesame oil

½ medium yellow onion, halved and thinly sliced

4 green onions, cut on the diagonal, plus more to garnish

½ cup diced carrots

½ cup sliced mushrooms

1 tsp grated ginger root

2 tbsp tamari or coconut aminos

6 cups cold cooked long-grain rice (such as jasmine or brown rice)

½ cup frozen peas

3 large eggs, beaten

1. Cut the pork chops into thin 1-inch (2.5cm) long slices and toss with the salt and pepper. In a large wok or large nonstick skillet, heat 2 tablespoons avocado oil over medium-high heat. Add the pork pieces and sauté until cooked all the way through and no longer pink in the middle. Remove from the skillet and set aside.

2. In the same pan, add the sesame oil, yellow onion, green onions, carrots, mushrooms, and ginger. Cook until tender-crisp and slightly chewy, about 5 minutes. Add the tamari and stir until well disbursed. Remove the vegetables from the pan and set aside.

3. Add the remaining 1 tablespoon avocado oil to the pan. Add the rice, increase the heat to high, and cook until slightly browned, stirring constantly.

4. Lower the heat to medium, add back the vegetables and pork, and add the frozen peas. Cook, stirring constantly, for 5 minutes.

5. Create a well in the middle of the rice mixture so that the pan is exposed. Pour the beaten eggs into the well and cook. Once cooked through, break up into pieces and stir throughout the rice mixture. Garnish with green onions and serve immediately.

Store it

Store leftovers in an airtight container in the refrigerator for up to 5 days or freeze individual portions in airtight containers for up to 3 months. Reheat in the microwave or on the stovetop.

Tip

Day-old rice that has been in the refrigerator works really well for this recipe. The rice will fry up better if cold and a little dried out.

I have adapted this pork tenderloin recipe from my mother-in-law to be gluten-free. It is so full of flavor and easy to make. This tenderloin is cooked on the grill and makes a great meal for those hot days when you don't want to turn on your oven. I love serving it alongside rice and a vegetable.

Linda's Luscious Pork Tenderloin

½ cup tamari or coconut aminos

½ cup rice wine vinegar (gluten-free)

2 tbsp sesame oil

2 tbsp honey

1 tsp grated ginger root

2 cloves garlic, minced

½ tsp lemon pepper seasoning

1 large or 2 small pork tenderloins (about 3lb/1.5kg total)

1. In a small bowl, whisk together the tamari, rice wine vinegar, sesame oil, honey, ginger, garlic, and lemon pepper seasoning until well combined.

2. Pour the sauce into a large resealable bag. Add the pork and marinate for 30 minutes at room temperature. Preheat the grill to medium heat, about 350°F (180°C).

3. Place the pork on the hot grill and discard the marinade. Grill for 14 to 16 minutes, turning every 3 to 4 minutes, until the internal temperature reaches at least 145°F (65°C) for a slightly pink middle, or a few minutes longer for well done.

4. Wrap the pork in foil and let it rest for 5 minutes. Cut on a diagonal, place on a serving dish, and pour any juices collected in the foil over the pork. Serve immediately.

Beef, mushrooms, cream sauce, and pasta come together in this classic dish that will soon become a regular on your table. The beef is slowly cooked in a rich, creamy sauce, giving it tons of flavor and making it super moist and tender. My husband loves anything with a good sauce, and this has become one of his favorites.

Classic Beef Stroganoff

9–12oz (225–340g) uncooked gluten-free pasta (such as large egg noodles by Jovial or brown rice pasta spirals by Tinkyada)

1 tbsp avocado oil

1½lb (680g) beef sirloin, cut into 1 x ½-in (2.5 x 1.25cm) pieces

¼ cup salted butter

1 yellow onion, halved and thinly sliced

8oz (225g) sliced white mushrooms

2 cups beef stock, divided

½ tsp salt, plus more to season

¼ tsp freshly ground black pepper, plus more to season

½ tsp dried thyme

2 tsp Worcestershire sauce (gluten-free)

¼ cup #1 All-Purpose Flour Blend (page 24)

1 tsp Dijon mustard

1 cup sour cream

1 tbsp chopped flat-leaf parsley

Paprika, to serve

1. In a medium pot, cook the pasta according to the package directions. Rinse immediately under cold water. Set aside.

2. In a large deep sauté pan, heat the oil over medium-high heat. Season the beef with salt and pepper. Brown the beef in the hot oil for 2 to 3 minutes. Remove the meat from the pan.

3. Add the butter to the meat juices in the pan and melt. Add the onions and mushrooms. Cook just until soft, about 5 minutes.

4. Stir in 1 cup beef stock, salt, pepper, thyme, and Worcestershire sauce. Add the meat back into the pan and stir. Bring to a boil, reduce the heat, cover, and simmer for 15 minutes.

5. In a small bowl, whisk the #1 All-Purpose Flour Blend, mustard, and the remaining 1 cup stock. Stir into the beef mixture. Bring to a boil and stir constantly for 1 minute.

6. Turn the heat to low and stir in the sour cream and parsley. Cook until heated through, but do not boil. Taste and season with more salt and pepper to taste. Sprinkle some paprika on top and serve immediately over the cooked pasta.

This recipe came about when we had leftover steak but I didn't want to just eat a leftover slice of meat. I absolutely love horseradish, so the creamy sauce in this recipe is heavenly to me. You can use leftover meat to make these sandwiches, or you can buy fresh. The flavor combination is unbelievable.

Steak Sandwiches
with Horseradish Cream Sauce

2 tbsp salted butter

1 tbsp avocado oil

1 yellow onion, sliced

1 lb (450g) London broil, tri-tip, or your favorite cut of beef

Salt and freshly ground black pepper, to taste

4–8 slices Muenster or provolone cheese

Easy White Sandwich Bread (page 113) or store-bought gluten-free bread or rolls (see the tip)

Horseradish Cream Sauce

⅓ cup mayonnaise

1 tsp stone-ground mustard

5 tsp prepared horseradish

1. Preheat a grill or a grill pan over medium-high heat. In a medium skillet, heat the butter and oil over medium-high heat. Add the sliced onions to the skillet and cook until very soft and slightly caramelized, about 15 minutes.

2. Meanwhile, season the meat with salt and pepper and grill until the desired doneness is reached, about 8 minutes per side for medium. Thinly slice the cooked meat.

3. Preheat the broiler. Lightly warm up or toast the bread. Spread the horseradish cream sauce on each slice of bread. Set the top slices of bread aside. Top the bottom slices of bread with slices of meat, the cooked onions, and finally the sliced cheese. Place the bottom piece with the meat, onions, and cheese a few inches under the broiler and cook until the cheese is melted.

4. Place the top piece of bread on top of each sandwich. Serve the sandwiches with more horseradish cream sauce on the side.

Horseradish Cream Sauce: In a small bowl, stir together the mayonnaise, mustard, and horseradish. Refrigerate until ready to use.

Tip

I like to use Udi's Gluten-Free Hot Dog Buns when making these sandwiches—it tastes like I'm eating a steak sandwich on a French roll!

Serves:
8–10 (makes about
5qt/4.75 liters)

Prep time:
20 minutes

Cook time:
2½ hours

My dad's chili, or Papa's Chili as it's known around our house, is the best chili around. It's amazing on top of baked potatoes, French fries, corn chips, or just straight out of a bowl. It is so meaty and hearty—a perfect meal on a chilly day.

Papa's Meaty Chili

2 tbsp avocado oil

2 Anaheim or poblano chiles

1 yellow onion, chopped

2 cloves garlic, minced

1 tsp salt, plus more to season

½ tsp freshly ground black pepper, plus more to season

2lb (1kg) sirloin steak or chuck roast, cut into bite-sized pieces

1 (15.5oz/440g) can diced tomatoes

2 cups beef stock

1 tsp chili powder

1 tsp ground cumin

2lb (1kg) ground beef

2 (15.5oz/440g) cans pinto beans, drained and unrinsed

1 (15.5oz/440g) can dark kidney beans, drained and rinsed

2 (15.5oz/440g) cans chili beans (such as pinto beans in mild chili sauce)

Sour cream, shredded cheese, tortilla chips, or Fritos (optional), to serve

1. In a large stockpot or Dutch oven, heat the oil over medium-high heat. While the oil is heating, slice the Anaheim chiles in half, discard the seeds, and dice. Add the diced chiles and onion to the pot, and sauté for 5 minutes, or until soft and translucent. Add the garlic, salt, and pepper, and cook for 30 seconds more.

2. Season the steak with salt and pepper and add to the pan. Cook just until browned, stirring often.

3. Stir in the diced tomatoes with the juices, beef stock, chili powder, and cumin. Bring just to a boil, reduce the heat to low, cover, and simmer for about 1 hour, or until the steak is tender.

4. Meanwhile, in a medium sauté pan, cook the ground beef over medium heat until no longer pink, breaking it up into little pieces.

5. To the stockpot, add the ground beef, along with the pinto beans, kidney beans, and chili beans. Stir to combine and simmer for an additional 1 hour. Season with salt and pepper to taste. Serve immediately with the desired toppings.

Slow Cooker Method: First follow steps 1 and 2 to sauté the chiles, onion, garlic, and sirloin in a large skillet. Add the mixture to a slow cooker, and brown the ground beef in the same skillet. Then add all of the ingredients to a slow cooker. Cook on low for 6 to 8 hours or on high for 3 to 4 hours.

Store it

Store in an airtight container in the refrigerator for up to 5 days or in the freezer for up to 6 months.

Tip

To make this red meat–free, substitute bite-sized pieces of chicken breast for the sirloin, ground turkey for the ground beef, and chicken stock for the beef stock.

Serves:
4

Prep time:
10 minutes

Cook time:
2 hours 20 minutes

This recipe came from my husband's grandma Joy and has been served at many family gatherings. We love it with mashed potatoes. I have adapted this recipe to taste as close to the original version as possible. Do not rush the cooking time. The low and slow cooking is what makes the meat so tender.

Grandma Joy's Swiss Steak

¾ cup #1 All-Purpose Flour Blend (page 24), divided

1 tsp salt, divided

4 tbsp avocado oil, divided

2lb (1kg) round steak (cut into 4–6 pieces)

1 yellow onion, halved and thinly sliced

3 cups chicken stock, divided

1½ tsp celery salt

⅛ tsp freshly ground black pepper

1 (12oz/340g) box condensed gluten-free cream of mushroom soup (such as Pacific)

½ cup heavy whipping cream

1. Preheat the oven to 300°F (150°C). In a medium shallow dish, stir together ½ cup #1 All-Purpose Flour Blend and ½ tsp salt.

2. In a large nonstick frying pan or an electric skillet, heat 3 tablespoons avocado oil over medium-high heat.

3. Dredge each piece of meat in the flour and brown both sides in the heated oil, about 2 minutes per side. Remove from the pan and transfer to a 9 x 13-inch (23 x 33cm) baking dish. Set aside.

4. Add the remaining 1 tablespoon avocado oil and the sliced onions to the pan and cook for about 5 minutes, or until soft.

5. Meanwhile, in a small bowl, stir together 2¾ cups chicken stock, celery salt, the remaining ½ teaspoon salt, pepper, and the remaining ¼ cup #1 All-Purpose Flour Blend.

6. Add the chicken stock mixture to the onions, and deglaze the bottom of the pan with a wooden spoon. Add the cream of mushroom soup and the heavy whipping cream and stir well. If too thick, add the additional ¼ cup chicken stock until it's the consistency of gravy.

7. Pour the gravy on top of the meat, cover, transfer to the oven, and bake for 2 hours. Let cool slightly, and then serve.

With all the flavors of enchiladas and the ease of a casserole, this recipe is great for those busy nights during the week, and any that is left over makes for a delicious lunch the next day. My mom has been making this recipe for as long as I can remember.

Mama's Enchilada Pie

1 tbsp avocado oil

1 small yellow onion, chopped

2 cloves garlic, minced

1lb (450g) ground beef or turkey

1 (10oz/285g) can red enchilada sauce (gluten-free; see the tip)

1 (8oz/225g) can tomato sauce

½ tsp salt

1 (4.5oz/130g) can chopped or sliced black olives, drained

8–10 corn tortillas, quartered

3 hard-boiled large eggs, chopped

¾lb (340g) shredded Monterey Jack cheese

Sour cream, guacamole or avocado slices, lime wedges, and hot sauce (optional), to serve

1. Preheat the oven to 350°F (180°C) and grease the bottom of an 8- or 9-inch (20 or 23cm) square casserole dish.

2. In a large pan, heat the oil over medium-high heat. Add the onions and sauté until soft, about 5 minutes. Add the garlic and cook for 30 seconds. Add the ground beef, breaking it up into small pieces, and cook until no longer pink in the middle. Drain off any fat.

3. Add the enchilada sauce, tomato sauce, salt, and olives to the pan. Stir until combined and remove from the heat.

4. Place half of the tortillas in the bottom of the pan, overlapping the pieces to cover the entire pan without any gaps. Pour half of the meat mixture over the tortillas and spread evenly, followed by half of the eggs and half of the cheese.

5. Repeat the layers, ending with the remaining cheese. Bake, uncovered, for 30 minutes. Let rest for 5 minutes and then serve with the desired toppings.

Tip

Read your labels! Most red enchilada sauces contain flour and aren't gluten-free. My favorite brand of gluten-free red enchilada sauce is Frontera.

Stir-fry typically contains soy sauce (which contains wheat), but this version uses tamari instead. The orange marmalade adds a touch of sweetness to balance out the ginger. Serve on top of rice and you'll be reminded of your favorite Chinese restaurant. My older son, a very picky eater, once said, "Mom, this is the best steak I've ever had!"

Chinese Takeout Beef & Broccoli Stir-Fry

1½lb (680g) broccoli, cut into bite-sized pieces
1lb (450g) flank steak, cut into 1 x ¼-in (2.5 x 0.5cm) slices
2 tbsp cornstarch, divided
1 clove garlic, minced
1 tsp grated ginger
½ tsp salt
Dash of freshly ground black pepper
1 tbsp avocado oil
1 tsp sesame oil
4 tbsp orange marmalade
3 tbsp sweet garlic chili sauce
¼ cup tamari or coconut aminos
¼ cup water
¼ cup roasted cashews
White rice, to serve

1. In a large pot, cover the broccoli pieces with about 2 inches (5cm) water. Cover and cook over high heat for 5 minutes.

2. In a medium bowl, toss the steak with 1 tablespoon cornstarch, garlic, ginger, salt, and pepper until the steak is thoroughly coated.

3. In a large skillet or wok, heat the avocado and sesame oil over medium-high heat. Add the steak and stir-fry for 4 to 5 minutes or until almost cooked through. Reduce the heat to medium.

4. In a small bowl, whisk together the remaining 1 tablespoon cornstarch, orange marmalade, sweet chili sauce, tamari, and water. Whisk until well combined.

5. Add the broccoli and sauce to the skillet. Mix well. Cover and simmer for 5 minutes, stirring frequently, until the sauce has slightly thickened. Stir in the cashews and serve over rice.

I grew up eating this lasagna. With gluten-free lasagna noodles or zucchini noodles, I can still enjoy one of my childhood favorites. The homemade meat sauce, Mom's Famous Meat Sauce, is the secret in this amazing lasagna. It is absolutely worth the time and effort.

Meaty Lasagna

10oz (285g) gluten-free lasagna noodles (such as Tinkyada), or 5–6 large zucchini, cut lengthwise into ¼-in (0.5cm) thick slices

2 large eggs, beaten

3 cups whole milk cottage cheese

½ cup freshly grated Parmesan cheese

1 tbsp dried parsley

1 tsp salt, plus more if using zucchini

½ tsp freshly ground black pepper

4½ cups Mom's Famous Meat Sauce (page 82) or another meat sauce

16oz (450g) mozzarella cheese, shredded

1. Preheat the oven to 375°F (190°C). If using pasta, cook the gluten-free noodles for 2 minutes less than the package directions (10 minutes total if using Tinkyada brand). Rinse immediately under cold water.

2. If using zucchini, sprinkle salt over the zucchini slices and place in a colander to drain for 15 minutes. Blot any excess moisture with paper towels before using. Make sure the zucchini is as dry as possible.

3. In a medium bowl, whisk the eggs. Add the cottage cheese, Parmesan, parsley, salt, and pepper. Stir until well combined.

4. Spread ½ cup meat sauce in the bottom of a 9 x 13-inch (23 x 33cm) dish. Layer half of the noodles or zucchini slices in the pan, overlapping them. Spread half of the cottage cheese mixture over the noodles, followed by one-third of the mozzarella cheese, and then top with 2 cups meat sauce. Repeat the layers using the remaining noodles, cottage cheese mixture, one-third mozzarella cheese, and 2 cups meat sauce. Spread the remaining ⅓ mozzarella cheese on top.

5. Bake for 45 minutes, or until bubbly and the cheese is melted and golden brown. Let rest for 10 to 15 minutes before serving.

Store it

Store in an airtight container in the refrigerator for up to 5 days, or cut the lasagna into individual portions, place in airtight containers, and freeze for up to 3 months. Thaw in the refrigerator, reheat in the microwave, or place directly in the oven from the freezer.

Makes:
2 dozen

Prep time:
10 minutes

Cook time:
25 minutes

A party would not be a party without my mom bringing her meatballs. They are definitely a party-pleaser and are great served out of a slow cooker, over a big plate of gluten-free spaghetti, or as an appetizer on a tray with toothpicks. They are awesome served soaking in Mom's Famous Meat Sauce (see the tip).

Homemade Meatballs

1 tbsp avocado or olive oil

1 small yellow onion, chopped

3 cloves garlic, minced

1lb (450g) ground beef

1lb (450g) ground pork

½ cup Homemade Breadcrumbs (page 25) or store-bought plain gluten-free breadcrumbs

¼ cup freshly grated Parmesan cheese

2 tbsp marinara sauce or Mom's Famous Meat Sauce (page 82)

2 tsp dried parsley

1 tsp dried basil

½ tsp salt

¼ tsp freshly ground black pepper

1 large egg, beaten

1. Preheat the oven to 375°F (190°C). Line a baking sheet with parchment paper. In a large sauté pan, heat the oil over medium-high heat. Sauté the onions until soft and translucent, about 5 minutes. Add the garlic and cook for 1 minute more.

2. Transfer the cooked onion and garlic to a large bowl. Add the ground beef, ground pork, Homemade Breadcrumbs, Parmesan, marinara sauce, parsley, basil, salt, pepper, and egg. Mix initially with a spoon, and then with your hands until combined; do not overmix or the meatballs will turn out tough.

3. Using a spoon, roll the meat mixture into 2-inch (5cm) balls. Place the meatballs on the prepared baking sheet and bake for 20 to 25 minutes. Remove from the oven and serve immediately.

Tip

To serve these as an appetizer with a sauce, once you've baked the meatballs, transfer them to a slow cooker with Mom's Famous Meat Sauce (page 82) to cover, or 32oz (950g) jarred marinara sauce, such as Rao's. Cook on low for 3 hours before serving.

Store it

Lay the meatballs out on a baking sheet and freeze. Once frozen, place them in a freezer bag or airtight container and freeze for up to 6 months. Thaw in the refrigerator, in the microwave, or place directly into a slow cooker with sauce and reheat on low for 6 hours.

Makes:
about 9 cups

Prep time:
10 minutes

Cook time:
1½ hours

My mom has been making this pasta sauce since I was a little girl. I never found a jarred sauce I liked as much as mom's. The longer the sauce simmers, the more flavorful it will be. When I make a batch, I always use it over spaghetti and meatballs first, and then in my Chicken Parmesan (page 54) or Meaty Lasagna (page 79).

Mom's Famous Meat Sauce

2 tbsp avocado oil, divided

1 small yellow onion, finely chopped

4 cloves garlic, minced

1lb (450g) ground beef or turkey

1 (30oz/850g) can tomato sauce

1 (6oz/170g) can tomato paste

2 (15oz/420g) cans Italian-style stewed tomatoes

1 tsp salt, plus more to taste

½ tsp freshly ground black pepper

1 tbsp dried basil

1 tbsp dried oregano

2 tbsp dried parsley

¼ tsp pure cane sugar

1. In a large Dutch oven or heavy-bottomed pot, heat 1 tablespoon avocado oil over medium heat. Add the onion and sauté for about 5 minutes, or until soft and translucent. Add the garlic and sauté for 1 minute more.

2. Add the remaining 1 tablespoon avocado oil, along with the ground beef or turkey, and cook, breaking it up into small pieces, until no longer pink.

3. Add the tomato sauce and tomato paste. Stir well to combine.

4. Pulse the stewed tomatoes in a blender a few times to break up the large pieces, and then add to the pot. (This step is optional, depending on whether or not you like large chunks of tomatoes in your sauce.)

5. Add the salt, pepper, basil, oregano, parsley, and sugar to the pot. Stir well. Bring just to a boil, turn down the heat to low, cover, and simmer for a minimum of 1 hour, or for the entire day. Salt to taste and serve.

Store it

Store in airtight containers in the refrigerator for up to 5 days. This sauce freezes well. I like to freeze it in multiple 8fl oz (235ml) containers; that way I always have some sauce ready and it can be used as an individual portion, or I can defrost a couple containers for the whole family.

This recipe is for my dad and father-in-law—meatloaf is each of their favorite meal! Add a side of mashed potatoes and gravy and they'd both be in heaven. This meatloaf is loaded with flavor and uses gluten-free crackers. It's crispy on the outside and moist on the inside without being mushy.

Meatloaf
with Balsamic Glaze

¾ cup crushed gluten-free saltine-style crackers
1 tbsp avocado oil
1 cup finely chopped onion
4 cloves garlic, minced
2 large eggs
2lb (1kg) ground beef
½ cup freshly grated Parmesan cheese
1 tsp dried parsley
3 tbsp ketchup
2 tbsp Worcestershire sauce (gluten-free)
½ tbsp Dijon mustard
1½ tsp salt
½ tsp freshly ground black pepper
½ tsp paprika

Glaze
½ cup ketchup
1 tbsp balsamic vinegar
3 tbsp light brown sugar
½ tsp garlic powder
¼ tsp onion powder
¼ tsp freshly ground black pepper
¼ tsp salt

1. Preheat the oven to 400°F (200°C). Make the glaze. In a small bowl, stir together all of the ingredients and set aside until needed.

2. Place the crackers in a resealable bag and use a rolling pin to crush the crackers into fine crumbs.

3. In a small pan, heat the oil over medium heat and sauté the onions until soft and translucent. Add the garlic and cook for 1 minute more. Set aside and let cool.

4. In a large bowl, whisk the eggs. Add the onions, ground beef, Parmesan, parsley, ketchup, Worcestershire sauce, mustard, salt, pepper, paprika, and cracker crumbs. Mix with your hands until just combined; do not overmix.

5. Transfer the meat mixture to a 9 x 5-inch (23 x 12.5cm) loaf pan and lightly press down. Brush half of the glaze evenly over the top of the loaf, reserving the other half for later.

6. Bake the meatloaf for 40 minutes. Remove the pan from the oven and spread half of the remaining glaze evenly over the top. Bake for an additional 20 to 30 minutes or until the internal temperature reaches at least 160°F (70°C).

7. Pour off any grease that has accumulated and reserve. Let rest for 10 minutes.

8. While the meatloaf is resting, make a sauce to serve. In a small pan, mix 2 tablespoons of the poured off juices from the pan with the remaining glaze. Simmer until heated through. Remove the loaf from the pan, slice, and serve with the sauce.

Tip

If you love the crispier outer edges of the meatloaf like I do, then prepare this recipe as mini loaves or in a cupcake pan. Bake the smaller loaves for 25 minutes, brush with half of the remaining glaze, and bake for 10 minutes more, or until the internal temperature reaches 160°F (70°C).

Flour-Free Sides & Soups

Roasted Broccolini............................86

Maple Bacon Brussels Sprouts...........88

Hawaiian Macaroni Salad 89

Smashed Sweet Potatoes
  with Easy Garlic Aioli.......................91

Mom's Cheesy Potatoes....................92

Cheesy Rice Casserole......................93

Oven "Fried" Zucchini.......................94

Phil's Firehouse Beans......................96

Grandma Helen's Split Pea Soup 97

Loaded Baked Potato Soup................99

Taco Soup......................................100

Mexican Pork Stew..........................101

Eating gluten-free is easier when you eat lots of veggies to fill up, but I get tired of plain, steamed broccoli over and over again. This roasted Broccolini recipe has so much flavor and is a nice change from the usual. My favorite part is the crispy Parmesan. It's prepared in one bowl and the baking sheet is lined, so it's easy to make and clean up.

Roasted Broccolini

3 bunches Broccolini
(about 1½lb/680g)

3 tbsp avocado oil or olive oil

1 tbsp fresh lemon juice

3 cloves garlic, minced

½ tsp salt

¼ tsp freshly ground
black pepper

½ cup grated Parmesan cheese,
divided

1. Preheat the oven to 425°F (220°C) and line a baking sheet with parchment paper. Wash and trim the Broccolini and pat dry with paper towels.

2. In a large bowl, toss the Broccolini with the oil until all the pieces are coated. Add the lemon juice and toss until well distributed.

3. Add the garlic, salt, pepper, and ¼ cup Parmesan. Toss until well combined.

4. Evenly spread the Broccolini on the prepared baking sheet. Sprinkle the remaining ¼ cup Parmesan on top.

5. Bake for 20 minutes, or until the desired doneness. Serve immediately.

Serves:
4

Prep time:
10 minutes

Cook time:
35 minutes

I grew up eating Brussels sprouts with canned cheese sauce poured on top—so good! When I tried to introduce Brussels sprouts to my family, they looked at me like I had lost it. No interest! Determined to cook a recipe my family would tolerate, I developed this salty, sweet, crispy dish. Not only do they tolerate it, but they actually really like it.

Maple Bacon Brussels Sprouts

1 lb (450g) whole Brussels sprouts
1½ tbsp avocado oil
½ tsp salt
Freshly ground black pepper, to taste
4 slices uncooked bacon
1 tbsp pure maple syrup

1. Preheat the oven to 425°F (220°C). Wash the Brussels sprouts and drain. Trim the ends, and cut the Brussels sprouts in half.

2. In a large bowl, toss the Brussels sprout halves with the avocado oil, salt, and pepper. Spread them out evenly on a parchment-lined baking sheet.

3. Roast the Brussels sprouts for 20 to 25 minutes or until crispy and golden brown, stirring once halfway through the cooking time.

4. While the Brussels sprouts are roasting, in a large pan, cook the bacon over medium heat until crispy. Turn off the heat, remove the bacon, and reserve 2 tablespoons rendered fat in the pan, draining the rest. Chop the bacon.

5. Once the Brussels sprouts are done roasting, heat the reserved 2 tablespoons bacon fat in the same sauté pan. Add the Brussels sprouts and toss to coat evenly. Add the chopped bacon and cook until heated through, 3 to 5 minutes.

6. Add the maple syrup and toss to coat. Cook for an additional 1 to 2 minutes. Serve immediately.

Tip ....

You can roast and cook the Brussels sprouts and bacon up to 1 day in advance and store in the refrigerator. When ready to serve, follow steps 5 and 6.

Makes:
about 10 cups

Prep time:
30 minutes, plus
2 hours to chill

Cook time:
10 minutes

As a child standing at the deli counter, I always chose macaroni salad for my side dish. After going gluten-free, a trip to Hawaii—where macaroni salad appeared at every turn—motivated me to make my own recipe. I spent a full week making Hawaiian macaroni salad until I perfected it, and perfection this salad is.

Hawaiian Macaroni Salad

1lb (450g) gluten-free brown rice elbow macaroni (such as Tinkyada)
¼ cup apple cider vinegar
2¼ cups whole milk, divided
2¼ cups mayonnaise, divided
2½ tbsp light brown sugar
1½ tbsp pickle juice (from a jar of pickles)
½ tsp freshly ground black pepper
¼ cup grated yellow onion
¾ cup grated carrot
¾ cup finely chopped celery
Salt, to taste

1. Bring a large pot of salted water to a boil and cook the pasta for 2 to 5 minutes less than the package instructions (10 minutes total if using Tinkyada). Drain and rinse under hot water immediately.

2. Pour the pasta back into the pot and add the vinegar. Stir until it's evenly distributed and absorbed. Cool for 10 minutes.

3. While the pasta is cooling, in a small bowl, whisk together 1½ cups milk, 1 cup mayonnaise, brown sugar, pickle juice, and pepper.

4. Add the milk and mayonnaise mixture to the pasta and stir until combined. Cool completely in the refrigerator, about 1 hour, stirring from time to time.

5. Add the onions, carrots, celery, remaining ¾ cup milk, and remaining 1¼ cup mayonnaise to the pasta. Mix until evenly distributed. Cover and refrigerate for at least 1 hour, stirring from time to time. It will be a little runny at first, but as the pasta absorbs the sauce, it will thicken up. Taste and add more salt if desired. Serve chilled.

Store it
Store in an airtight container in the refrigerator for up to 5 days.

Tips
For day-to-day use, I normally use an avocado oil-based mayonnaise. However, for this recipe I have found that Best Foods brand tastes best.

This recipe is great to make a day in advance because it tastes better the longer it sits.

Serves:
6

Prep time:
10 minutes

Cook time:
1 hour

The combination of sweetness from the potatoes with salty tartness from the aioli is like a match made in heaven. I prefer to roast my garlic, but raw garlic works just as well. The white-fleshed sweet potatoes are just slightly sweet, so if you normally don't prefer sweet potatoes, give this dish a try—it might change your mind!

Smashed Sweet Potatoes
with Easy Garlic Aioli

3 large white-fleshed sweet
   potatoes (about 2lb/1kg)
1 tsp salt, plus more to season
Olive oil, to brush
Freshly ground black pepper,
   to taste

Easy Garlic Aioli
⅓ cup mayonnaise
1 tbsp olive oil
1½ tsp fresh lemon juice
1 tbsp chopped chives
¼ tsp salt
½–1 tsp chopped capers
2 cloves minced garlic or
   roasted and smashed
   (see the note)
Freshly ground black pepper,
   to taste

1. Slice the unpeeled potatoes into ½-inch (1.25cm) rounds.

2. Bring a large pot of water to a boil over high heat. Add the salt and the sliced potatoes. Gently boil for 20 to 25 minutes or until very soft. Drain the potatoes and let cool.

3. Heat the oven to 425°F (220°C) and arrange the cooled potato slices on a parchment-lined baking sheet. Using a fork, gently smash the potatoes, keeping the skin intact as much as possible.

4. Brush olive oil onto each potato slice, and then sprinkle salt and pepper on each slice. Bake for 15 minutes.

5. Gently flip each potato slice. Brush with more olive oil and sprinkle with more salt and pepper. Bake for an additional 15 minutes. If you would like them extra crispy, place the pan on the top rack and broil for 1 to 2 minutes, watching them closely to prevent burning. Serve the potato slices immediately with the aioli.

Easy Garlic Aioli: In a small bowl, whisk together the mayonnaise, olive oil, lemon juice, chives, salt, capers, garlic, and a dash of pepper. Whisk until well combined. Refrigerate until ready to serve.

Roasted Garlic: Preheat the oven to 400°F (200°C). Peel off any loose skin that is hanging off of the entire bulb, but be sure to leave the skin on each individual clove. Keeping the entire bulb intact, cut ¼ to ½ inch (0.5–1.25cm) off the top, exposing the inside of each clove. Place the bulb on a piece of foil. Drizzle a small amount of olive oil over the entire bulb. Enclose the bulb with the foil and bake for 30 to 40 minutes or until the cloves are extremely soft and spreadable. This recipe only calls for 2 cloves garlic; use the extra roasted garlic cloves for another use, such as spreading on warmed bread.

Serves:
8

Prep time:
20 minutes

Cook time:
50 minutes

My mom has been making this recipe for as long as I can remember, and it is not Christmas or Easter without this side dish on the table. This recipe is my absolute favorite way to eat potatoes. I think this dish is exceptional with ham for dipping in the cheesy sauce.

Mom's Cheesy Potatoes

1 tsp salt, divided

1 small onion, chopped

5 cups russet potatoes (about 3½lb/1.6kg), peeled and cut into ½-in (1.25cm) cubes

5 tbsp salted butter

1 clove garlic, minced

4 tbsp #1 All-Purpose Flour Blend (page 24)

2 cups whole milk

Dash of freshly ground black pepper

12oz (340g) sharp Cheddar cheese, grated

1. Preheat the oven to 375°F (190°C). Bring a large pot of water to a boil. Add ½ teaspoon salt, the chopped onion, and the potatoes. Cook for 10 minutes. Drain and rinse under cold water.

2. In a large saucepan, melt the butter over medium heat. Sauté the garlic until fragrant, about 30 seconds. Add the flour and stir for 30 seconds. Add the milk and cook, stirring constantly, until the sauce boils.

3. Add the remaining ½ teaspoon salt, pepper, and the Cheddar. Stir until the cheese is melted. Add the potatoes and stir to combine.

4. Pour the contents into a 2½ quart (2.5 liter) dish and bake, uncovered, for 30 minutes, or until bubbly and the potatoes are tender when poked with a fork. Let sit for 5 to 10 minutes before serving.

Tip ....

These potatoes are not only amazing served alongside ham, but also Brussels sprouts, asparagus, or broccoli. The vegetables taste amazing dipped in the cheese sauce.

Serves:
10

Prep time:
10 minutes

Cook time:
45 minutes

This is another recipe from my mother-in-law that is served at almost every holiday dinner or family barbecue. It is naturally all gluten-free, but it is loved by so many that I just had to include it in this book. I love when some is left over and I get to eat it for lunch the next day.

Cheesy Rice Casserole

2 cups uncooked long-grain white rice

16oz (450g) sour cream

1 (7oz/200g) can diced mild green chiles

¼–½lb (115–225g) Cheddar cheese, shredded (depending on desired cheesiness)

½lb (225g) Monterey Jack cheese, shredded

1. Preheat the oven to 350°F (180°C). Cook the rice according to package directions.

2. In a small bowl, stir together the sour cream and diced chiles.

3. Grease a 2½ quart (2.5 liter) dish. Evenly spread out a layer of half of the rice and lightly press down. Spread half of the sour cream mixture on top of the rice. Sprinkle half of both cheeses on top of the sour cream. Repeat the layers once more, using the remaining rice, sour cream, and then cheese.

4. Bake for 30 to 35 minutes or until the cheese is melted and bubbly. Serve immediately.

Serves:
4–6

Prep time:
20 minutes

Cook time:
20 minutes

A's Burgers, a fast-food restaurant in our town, has the best fried zucchini, especially when dipped in their ranch dressing. Growing up we would go to A's Burgers about once a week just for this side. My recipe is not only gluten-free, but also baked instead of fried so you can enjoy your "fried" zucchini without the guilt.

Oven "Fried" Zucchini

3 medium zucchini, cut into ¼-in (0.5cm) thick rounds

½ cup #1 All-Purpose Flour Blend (page 24)

3 large eggs

2 cups Homemade Breadcrumbs (page 25) or store-bought plain gluten-free breadcrumbs

½ cup freshly grated Parmesan cheese

2 tsp dried parsley

2 tsp salt

½ tsp freshly ground black pepper

1 tsp garlic powder

Avocado oil or other light cooking spray, to coat

1 batch Ranch Dressing (page 52) or another store-bought dipping sauce, to serve

1. Preheat the oven to 400°F (200°C). Line two baking sheets with parchment paper.

2. Prepare three shallow dishes. In the first, place the #1 All-Purpose Flour Blend. In the second, beat the eggs. In the third, stir together the Homemade Breadcrumbs, Parmesan, parsley, salt, pepper, and garlic powder.

3. Coat the zucchini slices in the flour, then in the eggs, and finally roll them around and press into the breadcrumbs to coat completely. Place each coated zucchini round on the prepared baking sheets. Once they're all prepared, spray the tops of the slices with cooking spray to help them crisp up.

4. Bake for 10 minutes. Flip and spray the other sides of each slice with cooking spray. Bake for an additional 10 minutes, or until the zucchini is soft and the breadcrumbs are golden brown and crispy. Serve immediately with ranch dressing for dipping

Air Fryer Method: Make these extra crispy in half the time using an air fryer. Prepare steps 1 to 4 as written. However, spray both sides of the zucchini before cooking. In the fryer basket, arrange the zucchini slices in an even layer (do not overlap), working in batches as needed. Cook at 400°F (200°C) for 9 minutes, and serve immediately.

It wouldn't be a family barbecue without Phil's beans. Phil, a longtime neighbor of my in-laws, was a fireman and would take whatever ingredients were available at the firehouse and make a pot of beans. From his creations came this recipe. It's not chili and it's not baked beans—it's "Phil's Beans," in a category of its own. They are amazing!

Phil's Firehouse Beans

2 (12oz/340g) packages Jimmy Dean sausage or another raw pork sausage roll (use 1 regular and 1 hot if you like it spicy)

1 (28oz/800g) can gluten-free baked beans (such as Bush's), undrained

1 (28oz/800g) can kidney beans, drained

1 (15oz/420g) can great northern beans, undrained

1 (15oz/420g) can chili beans in chili sauce (such as Ranch Style Beans with Jalapeño Peppers), undrained

1 yellow onion, chopped

8oz (225g) mushrooms (white or brown), sliced

3 stalks celery, chopped

¼ cup firmly packed light brown sugar

⅓ cup ketchup

2 tbsp yellow mustard

1. In a large skillet, brown the sausage meat, breaking it up into small pieces. Drain off the fat. Add the sausage to a slow cooker.

2. Add all of the remaining ingredients to the slow cooker. Cover and cook on low for 4 to 6 hours. Serve immediately.

Store it

Store in an airtight container in the refrigerator for up to 5 days or in the freezer for up to 3 months. Reheat on the stove.

Tip

If you want to speed up the cook time after browning the sausage, add all of the ingredients to a large stockpot and simmer for 2 to 3 hours.

Serves:
at least 20 people
as an appetizer

Prep time:
15 minutes

Cook time:
4 hours

You knew what day it was when you walked in the house and smelled this soup—my husband's grandma Helen was famous for her split pea soup on Christmas Eve. She would start cooking it when she woke up, and it would simmer all day. She always served it as an appetizer while the finishing touches were being put on the dinner.

Grandma Helen's Split Pea Soup

14oz (400g) bag dried green split peas
2 cups chicken stock
10 cups filtered water
1 smoked ham hock
1 yellow onion, chopped
½ tsp garlic powder
½ tsp dried oregano
½ tsp freshly ground black pepper
1 bay leaf
1½ cups thinly sliced carrots
1 cup chopped celery

1. In a large stockpot, combine the peas, chicken stock, water, ham shank, onion, garlic powder, oregano, pepper, and bay leaf.

2. Cook, uncovered, for 1½ hours at a rolling boil, stirring occasionally.

3. Remove the ham shank, trim off any meat, and chop the meat. Return the ham pieces to the pot.

4. Stir in the celery and carrots. Simmer over low heat, covered, for 2½ hours or for the remainder of the day. Serve hot.

Store it

Store in an airtight container in the refrigerator for up to 5 days or freeze individual portions in airtight containers for up to 3 months. Reheat on the stove or in the microwave.

Tips

The longer this soup simmers, the more it will thicken. If you like your split pea soup on the thicker side, then be sure to simmer it for as long as possible.

If you like your soup extra meaty, chop 1 to 2 ham steaks and add it with the carrots and celery.

Serves:
8

Prep time:
15 minutes

Cook time:
45 minutes

A loaded baked potato with sour cream, bacon, chives, and Cheddar cheese is one of my favorite things to eat for dinner. This soup combines all of these flavors into one giant pot. The soup is the ultimate comfort food.

Loaded Baked Potato Soup

12oz (340g) bacon, diced
¾ cup chopped yellow onion
½ cup salted butter
½ cup #1 All-Purpose Flour Blend (page 24)
4 cups chicken stock
4 cups whole milk
2lb (1kg) russet potatoes, peeled and cubed
4 green onions, thinly sliced, divided
1 cup diced cooked ham
3½ cups shredded sharp Cheddar cheese, divided
1 cup sour cream
1 tsp salt
½ tsp freshly ground black pepper

1. Heat a large stockpot or Dutch oven over medium-high heat. Add the bacon pieces and cook until crispy. Remove the bacon and drain off all but 1 tablespoon fat.

2. Cook the onion in the bacon fat for about 5 minutes, or until translucent.

3. Add the butter and melt. Whisk in the #1 All-Purpose Flour Blend and cook, whisking constantly, for 1 minute.

4. Gradually whisk in the chicken stock and milk. Cook, whisking constantly, until slightly thickened, 1 to 2 minutes. Stir in the potatoes, half of the green onions, and the diced ham.

5. Bring to a boil, reduce the heat, and simmer, covered, for 15 to 20 minutes or until the potatoes are tender when pierced with a fork.

6. Stir in 2½ cups Cheddar, sour cream, and half of the bacon. Season with salt and pepper to taste. Serve immediately topped with the remaining green onions, bacon, and Cheddar.

Have you ever craved the flavors of Mexican food but wanted the comfort of a bowl of soup? This recipe is exactly what you're seeking. My mother-in-law introduced it to me, and I made a few changes to make it gluten-free. This one-pot meal is easy to make, and everyone can customize their own bowl with an array of toppings.

Taco Soup

1 tbsp avocado or olive oil

1 cup chopped yellow onion

2lb (1kg) ground beef or turkey

1 (14.5oz/410g) can Mexican-style stewed tomatoes

2 (15.5oz/440g) cans pinto beans, undrained

1 (15.5oz/440g) can black beans, undrained

1 (15.5 oz/440g) can kidney beans, drained

1 (15.5 oz/440g) can whole kernel corn, drained

1 (14.5oz/410g) can diced tomatoes, undrained

1 (14.5z/410g) can diced tomatoes with green chiles, undrained

1 (4.5oz/130g) can diced green chiles

1 (4oz/110g) can sliced black olives, drained

2 tbsp Homemade Taco Seasoning or store-bought gluten-free taco seasoning

1 (1oz/25g) package ranch salad dressing mix (gluten-free; such as Simply Organic)

Shredded Monterey Jack or Cheddar cheese, sour cream, jalapeños, cilantro, and tortilla chips (optional), to serve

1. In a large stockpot or Dutch oven, heat the oil over medium heat. Add the onion and ground beef and cook until the meat is no longer pink, breaking it up into small pieces.

2. While the meat is cooking, put the stewed tomatoes with the juices in a food processor or blender. Pulse a few times to break up the large pieces of tomato.

3. To the stockpot, stir in the stewed tomatoes, pinto beans, black beans, kidney beans, corn, diced tomatoes, diced tomatoes with green chiles, green chiles, black olives, taco seasoning, and ranch salad dressing mix. Simmer, covered, over low heat for 1 hour. Serve immediately with the desired toppings.

Slow Cooker Method: First cook the meat and onions in a sauté pan, and then add to a slow cooker. Stir in the remaining ingredients. Cook on low for 5 to 6 hours or on high for 2 to 3 hours.

Store it ....

Store in airtight containers in the refrigerator for up to 5 days or freeze individual portions in airtight containers for up to 3 months. Reheat on the stove or in the microwave.

Homemade Taco Seasoning:

4 tsp ground cumin	1 tsp dried granulated garlic	4 tsp dried oregano
4 tsp paprika	1 tsp chili powder	1 tsp freshly ground
2 tsp dried ground onion	½ tsp cayenne (or more if you	black pepper
2 tsp garlic salt	prefer spicy)	2 tsp pure cane sugar (optional)

In a small bowl, mix together all of the ingredients. This recipe makes about 1 cup. I always have it on hand for whenever we make tacos because many packaged seasonings have added preservatives.

Serves:
8–10

Prep time:
10 minutes

Cook time:
1 hour

This twist on your typical stew has a bit of a Mexican flare to it. The cumin and diced green chiles provide the perfect blend of flavors. Like chili, it is fun to set up a topping bar when serving this soup. It tastes great with sour cream, shredded Monterey Jack cheese, cilantro, jalapeños, or avocados on top.

Mexican Pork Stew

2 tbsp avocado or olive oil, divided

1½–2lb (680g–1kg) pork loin, cut into 1-in (2.5cm) pieces

1 tbsp #1 All-Purpose Flour Blend (page 24)

½ yellow onion, chopped

3 cloves garlic, minced

½ cup dry white wine (or chicken stock)

6 cups chicken stock

1 bay leaf

2 tsp salt

½ tsp freshly ground black pepper

2 (4oz/110g) cans diced green chiles, undrained

1 cup sliced carrots

1½lb (680g) russet potatoes, white flesh sweet potatoes, or turnips

1 (15oz/420g) can pinto beans, drained

1 (15oz/420g) can great northern beans, drained

1 tsp dried thyme

½ tsp ground cumin

½ tsp ground coriander

1 tsp dried oregano

1 bunch kale (optional), chopped

Shredded Monterey Jack cheese, sour cream, cilantro, chopped avocado, and chopped jalapeños (optional), to serve

1. In a large stockpot or Dutch oven, heat 1 tablespoon oil over medium-high heat. In a large bowl, season the pork with salt and pepper, and toss to combine. Add the #1 All-Purpose Flour Blend and toss to thoroughly coat. Brown the pork in the hot oil.

2. Remove the pork from the pot. Add the remaining 1 tablespoon oil and sauté the onions for about 5 minutes, or until translucent. Add the garlic and cook for 1 minute more.

3. Add the wine and deglaze the bottom of the pan. Add the stock, bay leaf, salt, pepper, green chiles, carrots, potatoes, pinto beans, great northern beans, thyme, cumin, coriander, and oregano, along with the pork.

4. Bring the soup to a boil, reduce the heat, and simmer, covered, for 40 minutes.

5. If using, add the kale and simmer for an additional 10 minutes. Serve immediately with the desired toppings.

Store it

Store in an airtight container in the refrigerator for up to 5 days or freeze individual portions in airtight containers for up to 3 months. Reheat on the stove or in the microwave.

Perfect Pizzas & Breads

Easy Peasy Pizza Crust 104

BBQ Chicken Pizza 105

Thai Chicken Pizza 107

Mexican Pizza 108

Cornbread 109

Garlic Butter Naan 110

Ancient Grain Sandwich Bread 112

Easy White Sandwich Bread 113

Focaccia 115

Hamburger Buns 116

Flour Tortillas 117

Makes:
1 (11-in/28cm) crust
or 2 (8-in/20cm) crusts

Prep time:
35 minutes

Cook time:
15 minutes

Frozen pizzas or those delivered to your home just aren't the same when gluten-free, and homemade options typically involve hours of labor. So, like most other foods I miss, I created my own. This crust is actually really easy to make and does not take long at all. It has also been approved and loved by both of my kids.

Easy Peasy Pizza Crust

1¼ cups brown rice flour, divided

1¼ tsp quick-rising yeast (or active dry yeast; see the tip)

1½ tsp salt

1 tsp Italian seasoning

2 tsp xanthan gum

½ tsp garlic powder

¼ tsp onion powder

2 tsp pure cane sugar

¾ cup warm water (105–110°F/40–43°C)

1 tbsp olive oil, plus more to brush

2 tsp apple cider vinegar

¾ cup tapioca flour

1. Preheat the oven to 425°F (220°C) with a pizza stone or baking sheet inside the oven. (If you prefer to use active dry yeast, you will need to proof the yeast now; see the tip.) In a stand mixer fitted with the paddle attachment or in a large bowl, whisk together ½ cup brown rice flour, quick-rising yeast, salt, Italian seasoning, xanthan gum, garlic powder, onion powder, and sugar until well combined.

2. Turn on the slowest speed, and add the warm water, olive oil, and vinegar. Slowly add the remaining ¾ cup brown rice flour and the tapioca flour. Mix on low speed for 1 to 2 minutes, or until the dough comes together and pulls away from the sides of the bowl. Let rest for 10 minutes.

3. Rub a little bit of olive oil on your hands to prevent the dough from sticking. Form the dough into a disk (or 2 disks if making personal pizzas) and place between two sheets of parchment paper. Roll the dough out into an ⅛- to ¼-inch (3mm–0.5cm) thick circle, about 11 inches (28cm) in diameter. Remove the top sheet of parchment paper. Using a fork, gently poke holes around the whole crust. Brush the entire pizza crust with olive oil. Cover the crust with the top sheet of parchment paper and let rest for 10 minutes.

4. Remove the top sheet of parchment. Using the bottom piece of parchment, transfer the crust onto the stone or baking pan, keeping the parchment under the crust.

5. Par-bake for 15 minutes. Remove the crust and immediately brush the edges with water. The crust is now ready for your favorite toppings.

6. Once you've added your toppings, brush the edges with olive oil and bake for 12 to 15 minutes or until the cheese is golden brown.

Tip

To proof active dry yeast, stir the yeast into ½ cup of the warm water, along with 1 teaspoon of the sugar. (Add the remaining sugar with the dry mixture and the remaining water with the wet ingredients). Let sit for 5 minutes, or until foamy. Add the yeast mixture along with the rest of the wet ingredients.

Store it

After you've par-baked and cooled the crust, store in an airtight container in the freezer for up to 3 months. When ready to use, put your toppings directly on the frozen pizza and then bake. No need to defrost first.

Makes:
1 (11-in/28cm) pizza

Prep time:
10 minutes

Cook time:
15 minutes

Once I eventually caved and tried a BBQ pizza, I was hooked. As soon as I developed my gluten-free pizza dough, BBQ chicken was the first pizza I created. The BBQ sauce, onion, and cilantro deliver a great combination of flavors. If you're looking to mix up pizza night, this is a great recipe to try.

BBQ Chicken Pizza

1 par-baked Easy Peasy Pizza
  Crust (page 104)
Barbecue sauce (gluten-free),
  to cover
2 cups grated mozzarella
  cheese, divided
½ cup cooked cubed chicken
1 tbsp chopped red onion
1 tbsp chopped cilantro
Olive oil, to brush

1. Preheat the oven to 400°F (200°C) with a pizza stone or baking pan inside the oven. Place the par-baked pizza crust on a piece of parchment paper for easy transfer. Spread the barbecue sauce all over the par-baked pizza crust, leaving a bit uncovered around the perimeter.

2. Top with 1½ cups mozzarella, chicken, onion, and cilantro. Sprinkle the remaining ½ cup mozzarella on top.

3. Brush olive oil around the outside edge of the crust. Place the pizza directly on the preheated pizza stone or baking pan. Bake for 12 to 15 minutes or until the crust is golden brown and the cheese is melted. Slice and serve hot.

Tip ....

Serve with a side of ranch dressing for dipping. This pizza would also taste great with shredded pork.

Serves:
1 (11-in/28cm) pizza

Prep time:
10 minutes

Cook time:
15 minutes

A famous California-based pizza company makes a Thai chicken pizza, and it was my favorite when I was still eating gluten. Here is my version of that pizza. The creamy gluten-free peanut sauce is quick and easy to make. The many different flavors and textures in this pizza all combine to create one delicious pie!

Thai Chicken Pizza

1 par-baked Easy Peasy Pizza Crust (page 104)
1½–2 cups grated mozzarella cheese
¾ cup cooked cubed chicken
1 small carrot, shredded
1 green onion, chopped
1 tbsp chopped cilantro
1 tbsp chopped peanuts
Olive oil, to brush

Peanut Sauce

¼ cup creamy peanut butter (unsweetened)
1 tbsp tamari or coconut aminos
⅛ tsp ground ginger
¼ tsp garlic powder
½ tbsp rice wine vinegar
1 tbsp light brown sugar
1 tsp sweet chili sauce (gluten-free)
1 tsp fresh lime juice
3 tbsp water

1. Preheat the oven to 400°F (200°C) with a pizza stone or baking pan inside the oven. Place the par-baked pizza crust on a piece of parchment paper for easy transfer. Prepare the peanut sauce. In a small bowl, whisk together all of the ingredients. If the sauce is too thick, slowly whisk in more water 1 teaspoon at a time until you reach the desired consistency.

2. Spread the peanut sauce all over the par-baked pizza crust, leaving a bit uncovered around the perimeter. Top with 1 to 1½ cups mozzarella (to preference), chicken, carrots, green onion, cilantro, and peanuts. Sprinkle the remaining ½ cup mozzarella on top.

3. Brush olive oil around the outside edge of the crust. Place the pizza directly on the preheated pizza stone or baking pan. Bake for 12 to 15 minutes or until the crust is golden brown and the cheese is melted. Slice and serve hot.

Tip

Dip the pizza in any leftover peanut sauce, a sweet chili sauce, or your favorite hot sauce.

Makes:
1 (11-in/28cm) pizza

Prep time:
10 minutes

Cook time:
15 minutes

This pizza is so versatile because you can use so many different ingredients, many of which I usually have on hand in my pantry. My kids like it with just beans and cheese, and my husband and I like to pack on the ingredients like a plate of loaded nachos. A build-your-own Mexican pizza is a fun meal to create with a group.

Mexican Pizza

1 par-baked Easy Peasy Pizza Crust (page 104)

⅔ cup refried beans

½–¾ cup grated Monterey Jack cheese

½–¾ cup grated Cheddar cheese

¾ cup cooked cubed chicken

2 tbsp black olives, chopped

1–2 tbsp chopped cilantro

1 Roma tomato, diced

1 green onion, chopped

Sour cream, salsa, pickled jalapeños, or guacamole (optional), to serve

1. Preheat the oven to 400°F (200°C) with a pizza stone or baking pan inside the oven. Place the par-baked pizza crust on a piece of parchment paper for easy transfer. Spread the beans all over the par-baked pizza crust, leaving a bit uncovered around the perimeter. Evenly sprinkle both cheeses on top of the beans.

2. Evenly top with the chicken, olives, cilantro, tomato, and green onions.

3. Brush olive oil around the outside edge of the crust. Place the pizza directly on the preheated pizza stone or baking pan. Bake for 12 to 15 minutes or until the crust is golden brown and the cheese is melted. Slice and serve hot with the desired toppings.

Tip ....

Consider adding red onions or substituting ground beef for the chicken.

Nothing goes better with a bowl of chili or stew than a slice of cornbread. This easy-to-make recipe is moist, sweet, and fluffy straight out of the oven—no butter and honey required (but of course I'm not judging)!

Cornbread

1 cup #1 All-Purpose Flour Blend (page 24)
1 cup cornmeal
1½ tsp xanthan gum
½ tsp salt
1 tsp baking powder
½ tsp baking soda
⅓ cup salted butter, melted
⅔ cup pure cane sugar
1 large egg
1 cup buttermilk

1. Preheat the oven to 350°F (180°C). Grease only the bottom of an 8-inch (20cm) square baking dish. In a large bowl, whisk together the #1 All-Purpose Flour Blend, cornmeal, xanthan gum, salt, baking powder, and baking soda until thoroughly combined.

2. In a medium bowl, whisk the melted butter with the sugar until thick and smooth. Add the egg and buttermilk and whisk until well combined.

3. Add the wet ingredients to the dry ingredients. Whisk until smooth. Pour the batter into the prepared baking dish and bake for 20 to 25 minutes or until a toothpick inserted into the center comes out clean.

4. Cool in the pan for at least 5 minutes before cutting. Serve immediately.

Store it

Store in an airtight container in the refrigerator for up to 5 days or in the freezer for up to 3 months. Thaw at room temperature, in a microwave, or wrapped in foil in the oven.

Tip

Fold in these optional add-ins before transferring to the baking dish: 1 to 2 chopped jalapeños, 1 cup shredded Cheddar cheese, 1 small can diced green chiles, or ½ cup chopped bacon.

Makes:
8–10

Prep time:
15 minutes, plus
1 hour to rise

Cook time:
20 minutes

Dipping warm bread in dips or sauces is something I miss terribly when eating out. Indian food is definitely not the same without a piece of naan to soak up the butter chicken or tikka masala sauce. I have been known to sneak in some garlicky naan to restaurants, and now you can sneak this recipe in with you, too!

Garlic Butter Naan

1 cup warm water
   (105–110°F/40–43°C)
2 tbsp honey
3½–4 cups #1 All-Purpose
   Flour Blend (page 24), plus
   up to ½ cup more as needed
1 (0.25oz/7g) package
   quick-rising yeast (about
   2¼ tsp)
1 tsp xanthan gum
2 tsp salt
½ tsp baking powder
⅓ cup plain yogurt
1 tbsp apple cider vinegar
1 large egg
⅓ cup salted butter
3 cloves garlic, minced
Avocado or olive oil, to brush

1. In a stand mixer fitted with the paddle attachment or in a large bowl, stir together the warm water and honey until the honey has dissolved.

2. In a medium small bowl, whisk together 3½ cups #1 All-Purpose Flour Blend, yeast, xanthan gum, salt, and baking powder. Mix into the warm honey water on low speed.

3. On low speed, add the yogurt, vinegar, and egg. Increase the speed to medium and continue to mix for 2 minutes. The dough will still be sticky but should pull away from the edges of the bowl. If the dough is too sticky and not pulling away from the sides at all, mix in more flour 1 tablespoon at a time until the dough just starts to pull away. Do not add more than ½ cup additional flour.

4. Grease a medium bowl with avocado or olive oil, and lightly grease your hands. Remove the dough from the mixing bowl and shape into a ball. Place the ball of dough into the greased bowl. Cover with a damp towel and let rise in a warm place for about 1 hour, or until almost doubled in size.

5. Toward the end of the rise time, prepare the garlic butter. In a small sauté pan over medium heat, melt the butter. Add the minced garlic and cook for 1 to 2 minutes. Remove the pan from the heat, strain, and discard the garlic. Set aside.

6. Once the dough is risen to almost double in size, remove from the bowl and place on a lightly floured surface. Divide the dough into 8 to 10 pieces (depending on the desired size). Roll each piece into a ball.

7. Heat a large cast-iron skillet over medium-high heat. With a rolling pin, roll out each ball on the lightly floured surface until slightly thinner than ¼-inch (0.5cm) thick. Brush both sides with the garlic butter.

8. Working one or two at a time, add the rolled-out dough to the hot skillet and cook for 1 minute, or until the dough starts to bubble and the bottom is lightly golden brown. Flip the dough and cook for an additional 30 to 60 seconds. Transfer the naan to a plate and cover with a paper towel. Repeat with remaining dough.

9. Keep covered until ready to serve. Serve warm or at room temperature.

Store it

Store in an airtight container, each piece separated by a layer of parchment, and freeze for up to 3 months. Thaw at room temperature or reheat in a toaster oven or in a skillet.

Tips

When the naan is still warm, brush with butter and sprinkle with garlic salt, chopped cilantro, or any other fresh herbs, if desired.

This naan tastes great dipped in hummus, tzatziki, or warm spinach or artichoke dip. Use in place of pita bread for a gyro.

Makes:
1 (9-in/23cm) loaf

Prep time:
20 minutes, plus
1½ hours to rise

Cook time:
45 minutes

I could eat a slice of white bread with butter for breakfast, lunch, dinner, and every once in a while, I decide a healthier option might be best. This ancient grain bread is soft and moist and tastes just like a slice of white bread, but with the health benefits of ancient grains.

Ancient Grain Sandwich Bread

2½ cups Ancient Grain Flour Blend (page 24)

½ cup #1 All-Purpose Flour Blend (page 24)

1 tsp salt

2 tsp quick-rising yeast

2½ tsp xanthan gum

1 large egg, room temperature

½ cup whole milk

⅔ cup hot water

3 tbsp salted butter, melted

¼ cup honey

1 tbsp apple cider vinegar

3 tbsp sesame seeds (optional)

3 tbsp raw sunflower seeds (optional)

3 tbsp pepitas (optional), roughly chopped

1. In a medium bowl, whisk together the Ancient Grain Flour Blend, #1 All-Purpose Flour Blend, salt, yeast, and xanthan gum.

2. In a stand mixer fitted with the paddle attachment or in a large bowl, beat the egg for 1 minute on medium-high speed.

3. In a small bowl, combine the milk and the hot water. Once combined, the liquid temperature should be between 105 and 110°F (40 and 43°C). If too hot, let it cool down, and if too cold, microwave for a few seconds.

4. Add the warm milk–water mixture, butter, honey, and vinegar to the egg, and beat on medium-high speed until combined.

5. Slowly beat in the flour mixture on low speed. Increase the speed to medium and beat for 3 minutes. The dough will be very sticky and thinner and less pliable than gluten-based dough.

6. If adding sesame seeds, sunflower seeds, and pepitas, add to the dough and beat for an additional 1 minute on medium speed.

7. Lightly spray only the bottom of a 9 x 5-inch (23 x 12.5cm) loaf pan with cooking spray. Evenly spread the dough into the loaf pan. If the dough is too sticky to spread with a spatula, wet your fingers and spread with your fingertips.

8. Cover with a greased sheet of parchment paper and set in a warm place to rise for 1 to 1½ hours or until the dough has risen to the top of the pan.

9. Toward the end of the rise time, preheat the oven to 350°F (180°C). Bake for 40 to 45 minutes. The bread is done when the internal temperature reaches 205 to 210°F (96–99°C).

10. When it is done baking, do not take the bread out of the oven. Turn off the oven and open the oven door. Let the bread slowly cool in the oven for 10 to 15 minutes before removing it.

11. Remove the bread from oven and let cool completely on a wire rack in the loaf pan. Remove from the pan, slice, and serve at room temperature or warmed up.

Store it

Once cool, slice the entire loaf and store in an airtight container, each slice separated by a layer of parchment. Store in the freezer for up to 3 months. Thaw at room temperature, or pop directly into the toaster.

Makes:
1 (8-in/20cm) loaf

Prep time:
20 minutes, plus
1½ hours to rise

Cook time:
45 minutes

As soon as someone finds out I'm a gluten-free baker, their first question is, "Do you have a white bread recipe?" A good gluten-free white bread is almost impossible to find in a store—they're usually crumbly and cardboard-like. This recipe is moist, soft, and will have you guessing whether or not it is really gluten-free.

Easy White Sandwich Bread

3 cups #1 All-Purpose Flour Blend (page 24)

2 tbsp pure cane sugar

1½ tsp salt

2 tsp quick-rising yeast (or active dry yeast; see the tip)

3 tsp xanthan gum

1 large egg

½ cup whole milk

⅔ cup hot water

¼ cup salted butter, melted

1 tbsp honey

1 tbsp apple cider vinegar

1. In a medium bowl, whisk together the #1 All-Purpose Flour Blend, sugar, salt, yeast, and xanthan gum.

2. In a stand mixer fitted with the paddle attachment or in a large bowl, beat the egg for 1 minute on medium-high speed.

3. In small bowl, combine the milk and the hot water. Once combined, the liquid temperature should be between 105 and 110°F (40 and 43°C). If too hot, let it cool down, and if too cold, microwave for a few seconds.

4. Add the warm milk–water mixture, butter, honey, and vinegar to the egg, and beat on low speed until combined. Slowly beat in the flour mixture on low speed. Increase the speed to medium and beat for 3 minutes.

5. Evenly spread the dough into an ungreased 8 x 5-inch (20 x 12.5cm) loaf pan. Cover with a greased sheet of parchment paper and set in a warm place to rise for 1 to 1½ hours or until the dough has risen to the top of the pan.

6. Toward the end of the rise time, preheat the oven to 350°F (180°C). Bake for 40 to 45 minutes. The bread is done when the internal temperature reaches 205 to 210°F (96–99°C).

7. When it is done baking, do not take the bread out of the oven. Turn off the oven and open the oven door. Let the bread slowly cool in the oven for 10 to 15 minutes before removing it.

8. Remove the bread from the oven and let cool completely on a wire rack in the loaf pan. Remove from the pan, slice, and serve at room temperature or warmed up.

Store it

Once cool, slice the entire loaf and store in an airtight container, each slice separated by a layer of parchment, and freeze for up to 3 months. Thaw at room temperature, or pop directly into the toaster.

Tip

To proof active dry yeast, stir the yeast into the ⅔ cup warm water (105–110°F /40–43°C), along with 1 teaspoon of the sugar. Do not mix the milk with this mixture. (Add the remaining sugar with the dry mixture and the milk with the wet ingredients). Let sit for 5 minutes, or until foamy. Add the yeast mixture along with the rest of the wet ingredients.

Makes:
1 (9-in/23cm) loaf

Prep time:
20 minutes, plus
1 hour to rise

Cook time:
25 minutes

I love the fluffy texture of focaccia bread, so I set out to create a version that is as good as its gluten counterpart. My oldest son is a picky eater, and the first time I made this recipe, he ate the entire loaf himself. The olive oil and seasonings give it great flavor, and it has just the right crispiness on the outside and fluffiness on the inside.

Focaccia

2 cups #1 All-Purpose Flour Blend (page 24)

1 tsp xanthan gum

1 tsp salt

1 tbsp pure cane sugar

1 (0.25oz/7g) package quick-rising yeast (about 2¼ tsp)

½ tsp dried thyme

¼ tsp onion powder

¼ tsp garlic powder

½ tsp dried basil

½ tsp dried oregano

1 large egg, room temperature

¾ cup warm water (105–110°F/40–43°C)

2 tsp apple cider vinegar

2 tbsp olive oil, plus more to grease

Chopped fresh herbs (such as basil, oregano, or parsley) or garlic salt (optional), to top

1. Generously grease only the bottom of a 9-inch (23cm) round or square springform or cake pan with olive oil.

2. In a medium bowl, stir together the #1 All-Purpose Flour Blend, xanthan gum, salt, sugar, yeast, thyme, onion powder, garlic powder, basil, and oregano.

3. In a stand mixer fitted with the paddle attachment or in a large bowl, beat the egg for 30 seconds on high speed. Briefly incorporate the warm water, vinegar, and oil.

4. On low speed, carefully add the flour mixture to the wet ingredients. Scrape down the sides and increase the speed to medium-high. Beat for 2 minutes.

5. Pour the dough into the prepared pan—it will be very sticky. Wet your fingertips with warm water and gently spread the dough evenly in the pan. Very gently create divots on the top with your fingers, if desired.

6. Cover with parchment paper and set in a warm place to rise. Let the dough rise for 30 minutes to 1 hour or until doubled in size. Do not let the dough rise more than double, or it will fall flat when baked. When the dough has almost completed its rise, preheat the oven to 400°F (200°C).

7. Gently spray or brush the top of the risen dough with olive oil (be careful not to deflate the dough) and sprinkle with herbs, if desired.

8. Bake for 20 to 25 minutes or until golden brown. When done baking, do not take it out of the oven. Turn off the oven and open the oven door. Let the bread slowly cool in the oven for 10 to 15 minutes before removing it. Slice and serve warm.

Store it

This bread is best when eaten fresh, but if you have any leftovers, store in an airtight container at room temperature for up to 2 days. Warm it in the oven or microwave to soften it up. You can also store in an airtight container in the freezer for up to 3 months and thaw on the counter.

Tips

Be sure the eggs are room temperature and that your water is the correct temperature. If the ingredients are too cold, the yeast will not activate and create a proper rise. This is also why you want to wet your fingers with warm water when spreading out the dough. Finally, allowing the bread to cool down slowly will help prevent your loaf from sinking after it's baked.

Makes:
8

Prep time:
30 minutes, plus
1 hour to rise

Cook time:
20 minutes

I get so tired of having my burger "lettuce wrapped"—a burger is just not a burger without a bun. Many of the gluten-free hamburger buns out there just don't hold up, crumbling and falling apart with a juicy patty on it. My hamburger bun recipe is so tasty you will feel like you are enjoying a real burger again!

Hamburger Buns

3 cups #1 All-Purpose Flour Blend (page 24)

½ cup sweet sorghum flour

1 tbsp quick-rising yeast

1½ tsp salt

3 tbsp pure cane sugar

2 tsp xanthan gum

¾ cup club soda

½ cup hot water

5 tbsp salted butter, softened, divided

2 large eggs

2 tsp apple cider vinegar

1. Line two baking sheets with parchment paper. In a stand mixer fitted with the paddle attachment or in a large bowl, whisk together the #1 All-Purpose Flour Blend, sorghum flour, yeast, salt, sugar, and xanthan gum.

2. In a small bowl, add the club soda to the hot water. Once combined, the liquid temperature should be between 105 and 110°F (40 and 43°C). If too hot, let it cool down, and if too cold, microwave for a few seconds.

3. Add the water, 2 tablespoons butter, eggs, and vinegar to the flour mixture. Start mixing on low speed, and gradually increase the speed to medium. Mix for 2 minutes.

4. Divide the dough into 8 equal pieces. Shape each piece into a ball and place on the parchment-lined baking sheets. If the dough is too sticky to work with, rub oil on your hands before rolling.

5. Flatten the balls into 3-inch (7.5cm) round disks, cover, and let rise for about 1 hour, or until nearly double in size.

6. Preheat the oven to 375°F (190°C). Melt the remaining 3 tablespoons butter. Brush half of the butter on the buns. Bake for 15 to 18 minutes or until golden brown.

7. Remove the buns from the oven and brush with the remaining melted butter. Cool the buns on a wire rack. Once cooled, slice and serve.

Store it

Store the sliced buns in an airtight container in the freezer for up to 3 months. To defrost, wrap in a paper towel and microwave for 30 seconds or thaw on the counter.

Tip

Brush with butter and grill or toast before using.

Makes:
8 (6–7-in/15.25–
17.5cm) tortillas

Prep time:
30 minutes

Cook time:
25 minutes

A soft, mild, gluten-free flour tortilla is difficult to find, and corn tortillas get old. Store-bought gluten-free flour tortillas have come a long way, but I'm yet to find one I like without processed ingredients. These homemade tortillas have just a few ingredients and are even Max-approved so my son can enjoy his favorite—quesadillas!

Flour Tortillas

2 cups #1 All-Purpose Flour
   Blend (page 24)
¼ cup tapioca flour
1 tsp salt
¼ tsp baking powder
1 tbsp pure cane sugar
½ tsp xanthan gum
2 tbsp Spectrum palm
   shortening
1 tsp apple cider vinegar
¾ cup ice-cold water

1. In a stand mixer fitted with the paddle attachment or in a large bowl, whisk together the #1 All-Purpose Flour Blend, tapioca flour, salt, baking powder, sugar, and xanthan gum.

2. Add the palm shortening. Mix on medium-high speed until the shortening is well dispersed and pea-sized crumbs have formed.

3. On low speed, add the vinegar and water. Increase the speed to medium and mix for 2 minutes.

4. Heat a cast-iron skillet or griddle pan over medium heat. Place the dough on a piece of parchment paper and divide into 8 equal pieces. Roll each piece into a ball. Place a damp paper towel over the balls of dough until ready to use.

5. Working one at a time, place one of the balls of dough between 2 sheets of parchment paper and roll out into a 6- to 7-inch (15.25–17.5cm) circle. If the dough begins to stick, dust a small amount of tapioca flour onto the parchment paper and dough.

6. Carefully transfer the rolled-out dough to the hot skillet. Cook for 1½ minutes, flip, and cook for an additional 1½ minutes. Transfer to a plate lined with a damp paper towel and cover with another damp paper towel. Continue with the remaining dough, placing a damp paper towel between each tortilla.

7. Once all of the dough has been cooked, serve immediately.

Store it

Store in an airtight container, each tortilla separated by a layer of parchment, and freeze for up to 3 months. To defrost, one at a time, place a tortilla between two damp paper towels and microwave for 20 seconds.

Tips

Placing the freshly cooked tortillas between the damp paper towels helps them stay soft and flexible. However, if you leave them between the damp paper towels for too long, the towels will begin to stick to the tortillas. Remove the tortillas from the towels before they are completely cooled to avoid this.

This recipe works great with a tortilla press for perfectly round and perfectly cooked tortillas.

Sweet Loaves, Muffins & Scones

The Pumpkin Bread
That Started It All..............................121

Banana Nut Bread..............................122

Christmastime Cranberry Bread.........123

Cinnamon Swirl Bread.....................124

Max's Snickerdoodle Muffins............125

Blueberry Muffins..............................126

Carrot Zucchini Muffins....................128

Morning Glory Muffins......................129

Grab 'n' Go Coffee Cake Muffins........130

Petite Vanilla Scones.........................131

Gruyère, Prosciutto &
Chive Scones......................................133

Afternoon Tea Blueberry Scones........134

Coffee Shop Maple Scones.................135

Makes:
1 (9 x 5-in/23 x 12.5cm) loaf

Prep time:
15 minutes

Cook time:
1 hour

I have this recipe to thank for starting my gluten-free baking craze and making me famous for gluten-free baked goods in my hometown. In the process of recreating my mom's Thanksgiving Bundt cake, the recipe turned into loaves of pumpkin bread. Before I knew it, I was selling it to stores around town. Once you try it, you'll know why.

The Pumpkin Bread That Started It All

1½ cups pure cane sugar

½ cup plus 2 tbsp light vegetable oil (such as avocado oil)

2 large eggs

8oz (225g) canned 100% pure pumpkin

½ tsp salt

1 tsp xanthan gum

1 tsp baking powder

½ tsp baking soda

½ tsp ground cinnamon

¼ tsp ground allspice

¼ tsp ground nutmeg

⅛ tsp ground cloves

1¾ cups #1 All-Purpose Flour Blend (page 24)

⅓ cup water

1. Preheat the oven to 325°F (170°C). In a stand mixer fitted with the whisk attachment or in a large bowl, whisk together the sugar and oil on medium speed. Add the eggs and whisk on medium-high speed until well combined. Add the pumpkin and whisk until well incorporated.

2. In a separate medium bowl, whisk together the salt, xanthan gum, baking powder, baking soda, cinnamon, allspice, nutmeg, cloves, and #1 All-Purpose Flour Blend.

3. Alternate stirring the dry ingredients and the water into the wet ingredients, starting and ending with the flour mixture. Stir until well combined.

4. Pour the batter into an ungreased 9 x 5-inch (23 x 12.5cm) loaf pan and bake for 1 hour, or until a toothpick inserted into the center comes out clean. Cool completely before slicing.

Store it

Store in an airtight container on the counter for up to 3 days or freeze for up to 3 months. Either freeze the whole loaf, or freeze slices individually. Thaw at room temperature.

Tip

This bread makes an incredible Thanksgiving dessert by spreading a layer of Cream Cheese Frosting (page 160) on top.

Makes:
1 (9 x 5-in/23 x 12.5cm) loaf

Prep time:
15 minutes

Cook time:
1½ hours

After my pumpkin bread became a hit at the local farmer's market, I wanted to expand my bread offerings. This banana nut bread is the second gluten-free bread recipe I ever created, and probably my husband's favorite when warmed up with butter. Serve this to family and friends, and no one will ever know it's gluten-free.

Banana Nut Bread

1⅔ cups #1 All-Purpose Flour Blend (page 24) or Ancient Grain Flour Blend (page 24)

1 tsp baking soda

1 tsp xanthan gum

¼ tsp ground cinnamon

½ tsp salt

1 cup pure cane sugar

2 large eggs, room temperature

⅓ cup light vegetable oil (such as avocado oil)

3 very ripe small bananas, mashed

2 tbsp sour cream

1 tsp pure vanilla extract

⅔ cup chopped pecans

1. Preheat the oven to 350°F (180°C) and grease only the bottom of a 9 x 5-in (23 x 12.5cm) loaf pan. In a small bowl, whisk together the #1 All-Purpose Flour Blend, baking soda, xanthan gum, cinnamon, and salt.

2. In a stand mixer fitted with the paddle attachment or in a large bowl, beat the sugar and eggs on medium-low speed for about 3 minutes, until light in color.

3. While on low speed, slowly drizzle the oil into the sugar-egg mixture, and then increase the speed to medium and beat until well combined.

4. Add the mashed bananas, sour cream, and vanilla into the wet ingredients, and beat on low speed until just combined.

5. Gently stir the dry ingredients into the wet ingredients, being careful not to overmix. Gently stir in the chopped pecans. Add the batter to the loaf pan. Bake for 50 to 60 minutes or until a toothpick inserted into the center comes out clean. (If using the Ancient Grain Flour Blend, you may need to add 10 to 20 minutes to your baking time.)

6. Let cool in the pan for 10 minutes, and then transfer to a wire rack to cool completely, or slice and serve warm with butter.

Store it

Store in an airtight container on the counter for up to 3 days or freeze for up to 3 months. Either freeze the whole loaf or freeze slices individually. Thaw at room temperature.

Makes:
2 (9 x 5-in/23 x 12.5cm) loaves

Prep time:
15 minutes

Cook time:
1 hour

My mom used to make cranberry bread every Christmas and give it to neighbors as presents. It felt like Christmastime the second I would smell or taste it. This gluten-free rendition is so amazing when warmed up and slathered with butter.

Christmastime Cranberry Bread

2 cups fresh cranberries (or thawed frozen cranberries)

2 cups pure cane sugar, divided

8oz (225g) cream cheese, softened

½ cup Spectrum palm shortening

3 large eggs

1½ tsp pure vanilla extract

1 tsp apple cider vinegar

2 cups #1 All-Purpose Flour Blend (page 24)

2 tsp xanthan gum

1 tsp baking powder

½ tsp baking soda

½ tsp salt

¼ tsp ground mace

1. Preheat the oven to 350°F (180°C) and lightly grease only the bottoms of 2 (9 x 5-in/23 x 12.5cm) loaf pans. In a food processor, pulse the cranberries until coarsely chopped. In a small bowl, stir the cranberries with 1 cup sugar.

2. In a stand mixer fitted with the paddle attachment or in large bowl, beat the cream cheese, shortening, and the remaining 1 cup sugar until well combined.

3. Starting on low speed, beat in the eggs one at a time, and then increase the speed to high and beat in the vanilla and vinegar.

4. In a separate large bowl, whisk together the #1 All-Purpose Flour Blend, xanthan gum, baking powder, baking soda, salt, and mace until combined.

5. Pour the flour mixture into the wet ingredients and mix on low speed until combined. Gently stir in the cranberries.

6. Pour the batter into the two loaf pans and bake for 50 to 60 minutes or until a toothpick inserted into the center comes out clean.

7. Cool for 10 minutes in the pans and then transfer to a wire rack to cool completely. Slice and serve.

Store it

Store in an airtight container on the counter for up to 3 days or freeze for up to 3 months. Either freeze the whole loaf, or freeze slices individually. Thaw at room temperature.

Makes:
1 (9 x 5-in/23 x 12.5cm) loaf

Prep time:
20 minutes

Cook time:
1 hour

If you love cinnamon rolls, then you will love this quick bread recipe. You dump all of the ingredients into one bowl and then beat the mixture. Easy peasy to make and very little cleanup!

Cinnamon Swirl Bread

2 cups #1 All-Purpose Flour Blend (page 24)

1 cup pure cane sugar

1 tbsp baking powder

1½ tsp xanthan gum

½ tsp salt

⅓ cup sour cream

¼ cup salted butter, melted and cooled

½ cup whole milk

2 large eggs

Cinnamon Swirl

¼ cup firmly packed light brown sugar

1 tsp ground cinnamon

⅓ cup chopped walnuts or pecans

Glaze

¾ cup powdered sugar

1 tbsp whole milk

½ tbsp light vegetable oil (such as avocado oil)

¼ tsp pure vanilla extract

1. Preheat the oven to 350°F (180°C) and lightly grease only the bottom of a 9 x 5-inch (23 x 12.5cm) loaf pan.

2. Prepare the cinnamon swirl. In a small bowl, stir together the brown sugar, cinnamon, and chopped nuts. Set aside.

3. In a stand mixer fitted with the paddle attachment or in a large bowl, combine the #1 All-Purpose Flour Blend, cane sugar, baking powder, xanthan gum, salt, sour cream, melted butter, milk, and eggs. Beat on low speed for 1 minute. Scrape down the sides of the bowl and beat on medium speed for 1 minute longer.

4. Pour one-third of the batter into the loaf pan. (The batter will be very thick and you will need to use your fingers to spread it in the pan.) Sprinkle half of the cinnamon swirl over the batter. Pour another one-third of the batter into the pan, spreading with your fingers, and sprinkle with the remaining cinnamon swirl. Pour in the remaining batter and spread evenly.

5. Using a skewer or long toothpick, gently cut through the batter to swirl the cinnamon swirl around. Bake for 45 minutes. Cover the loaf with foil and bake for an additional 15 minutes, or until a toothpick inserted into the center comes out clean.

6. Pour the glaze over the hot bread while still in the pan. Let cool completely in the pan before slicing. Serve the slices at room temperature, or warm them up and serve with butter.

   Glaze: In a small bowl, stir together the powdered sugar, milk, oil, and vanilla.

Store it

Store in an airtight container on the counter for up to 3 days or freeze the slices individually wrapped for up to 3 months. Thaw at room temperature.

Makes:
16–18

Prep time:
20 minutes

Cook time:
25 minutes

These are the only muffins my son Max will ever eat. They taste just like snickerdoodle cookies—light, fluffy, and full of cinnamon-sugar sweetness. I love to serve these muffins to my kids as dessert, especially with butter.

Max's Snickerdoodle Muffins

2¼ cups #2 All-Purpose Flour Blend (page 24)

1½ tsp xanthan gum

½ tsp ground cinnamon

½ tsp salt

¾ tsp baking powder

¾ tsp baking soda

¾ tsp cream of tartar

1 cup salted butter, softened

1 cup pure cane sugar

2 large eggs, room temperature

1 tsp apple cider vinegar

2 tsp pure vanilla extract

1 cup sour cream

Topping

⅓ cup pure cane sugar

3 tbsp light brown sugar

1 tsp ground cinnamon

3 tbsp salted butter, melted

1. Preheat the oven to 350°F (180°C) and lightly grease the muffin tins (do not use muffin liners). In a large bowl, whisk together the #2 All-Purpose Flour Blend, xanthan gum, cinnamon, salt, baking powder, baking soda, and cream of tartar.

2. In a stand mixer fitted with the paddle attachment or in a large bowl, cream the butter and sugar on high speed for 3 minutes or until light and fluffy.

3. Add the eggs one at a time, beating on medium-high speed for 30 seconds between each addition. Add the vinegar, vanilla, and sour cream, and beat on medium-low speed until combined, scraping down the sides as necessary.

4. Add the wet ingredients to the flour mixture and stir just until combined—the batter will be thick. Using a ¼ cup measuring cup or ice cream scoop, fill each muffin cup about two-thirds full. Bake for 25 minutes, or until the muffins spring back when lightly touched and a toothpick inserted into center comes out clean.

5. While the muffins are baking, in a small bowl, make the topping. Stir together the cane sugar, brown sugar, and cinnamon until well combined.

6. Remove the muffins from the oven when done baking and leave in the pans until cool enough to touch. While the muffins are still warm, working one at a time, lightly brush the top of the muffin with butter and roll in the cinnamon-sugar mixture. Cool completely on a wire rack before serving.

Store it

Store in an airtight container in the refrigerator for up to 1 week or freeze for up to 3 months. Thaw at room temperature or reheat in the microwave.

Tip

A silicone muffin mold makes it very easy to pop the muffins right out.

Makes:
14

Prep time:
20 minutes

Cook time:
30 minutes

These muffins are so soft and moist that no one will ever know they are gluten-free. The crumb topping gives them a perfect amount of sweetness. Adding a touch of butter to your warm blueberry muffins makes them unbelievably scrumptious.

Blueberry Muffins

2 cups plus 1 tbsp #1 All-Purpose Flour Blend (page 24), divided

1 cup pure cane sugar

½ tsp salt

2 tsp baking powder

2 tsp xanthan gum

2 large eggs

⅓ cup light vegetable oil (such as avocado oil)

1 tsp apple cider vinegar

½ cup whole milk

½ cup sour cream

1 cup fresh or frozen blueberries

Topping

½ cup firmly packed light brown sugar

½ cup #1 All-Purpose Flour Blend (page 24)

½ tsp xanthan gum

¼ tsp salt

¼ tsp ground cinnamon

3 tbsp salted butter, firm and cut into small pieces

1. Preheat the oven to 375°F (190°C) and line the muffin pans with paper liners. Prepare the topping. In a medium bowl, stir together the brown sugar, #1 All-Purpose Flour Blend, xanthan gum, salt, and cinnamon. Cut in the butter with a pastry cutter or a fork until pea-sized crumbs are formed. Squeeze the mixture together with your hands and then break it up to form crumbs. Set aside.

2. In a large bowl, stir together 2 cups #1 All-Purpose Flour Blend, sugar, salt, baking powder, and xanthan gum until combined.

3. In a separate medium bowl, whisk the eggs, oil, vinegar, and milk until combined. Stir the wet ingredients into the dry ingredients just until combined, being careful not to overmix.

4. Gently stir in the sour cream. Toss the blueberries with the remaining 1 tablespoon All-Purpose Flour Blend before mixing in; this will prevent them from sinking to the bottom. Fold in the blueberries.

5. Using a ¼ cup measuring cup or ice cream scoop, fill each muffin cup about two-thirds full. Top the muffins evenly with the crumb topping. Bake for 28 to 30 minutes or until a toothpick inserted into the center comes out clean. Let cool in the pan for 5 minutes. Serve warm.

Store it

Store in an airtight container in the refrigerator for up to 5 days or in the freezer for up to 3 months. Thaw at room temperature or reheat in the microwave.

Makes:
12

Prep time:
20 minutes

Cook time:
30 minutes

Need to sneak some additional vegetables into your diet? These muffins give you a yummy way to do just that. Carrot Zucchini Muffins are a great school or work day breakfast when everyone is in a hurry.

Carrot Zucchini Muffins

1¼ cups #1 All-Purpose Flour Blend (page 24)

¼ cup firmly packed light brown sugar or coconut sugar

⅓ cup pure cane sugar

1 tsp ground cinnamon

1½ tsp baking powder

¼ tsp salt

1 tsp xanthan gum

½ cup old-fashioned rolled oats (certified gluten-free)

2 large eggs

3 tbsp salted butter, melted

1 tsp pure vanilla extract

1 tsp apple cider vinegar

½ cup sour cream

2 tbsp pure maple syrup

½ cup grated zucchini

½ cup grated carrots

4 tbsp raw sugar

1. Preheat the oven to 350°F (180°C) and line the muffin pans with paper liners. In a large bowl, stir together the #1 All-Purpose Flour Blend, brown sugar, cane sugar, cinnamon, baking powder, salt, and xanthan gum until well combined. Stir in the oats.

2. In a separate medium bowl, whisk together the eggs, melted butter, vanilla, vinegar, sour cream, and syrup. Add the wet ingredients to dry ingredients, and stir until just combined, being careful not to overmix. The batter will be thick and lumpy.

3. Add the zucchini and carrots, and stir until just incorporated. Using a ¼ cup measuring cup or ice cream scoop, fill each muffin cup about two-thirds full.

4. Bake for 25 to 30 minutes or until a toothpick inserted into the center comes out clean. Cool in the pan for 5 minutes, and then transfer to wire rack to cool completely, or serve warm with butter.

Store it

Store in an airtight container in the refrigerator for up to 3 days or in the freezer for up to 3 months. Thaw at room temperature or reheat in the microwave.

Makes:
about 2 dozen

Prep time:
30 minutes

Cook time:
35 minutes

These muffins are full of fruits and vegetables, making them substantial enough for starting your day right, plus they're not very sweet. They will definitely fill your tummy. The Morning Glory Muffin gets its name from the café where it originated—Morning Glory in Nantucket. These muffins will make your morning glorious, too!

Morning Glory Muffins

½ cup canned crushed pineapple

1 cup coconut sugar

¾ cup Ancient Grain Flour Blend (page 24)

¾ cup #1 All-Purpose Flour Blend (page 24)

2 tsp ground cinnamon

1 cup old-fashioned rolled oats (certified gluten-free)

2 tsp xanthan gum

2 tsp baking soda

½ tsp salt

½ cup unsweetened shredded coconut

½ cup finely chopped dried apricots (unsulfured and unsweetened)

1 apple, peeled and grated

2 cups grated carrots

½ cup chopped pecans

3 large eggs

1 tsp apple cider vinegar

1 cup sour cream

1 tsp pure vanilla extract

¼ cup pure maple syrup

Raw sugar or coconut sugar, to top

1. Place the pineapple in a strainer placed over a bowl to drain very well. Set aside until ready to use. Preheat the oven to 350°F (180°C) and line the muffin pans with paper liners.

2. In a large bowl, whisk together the coconut sugar, Ancient Grain Flour Blend, #1 All-Purpose Flour Blend, cinnamon, oats, xanthan gum, baking soda, and salt.

3. Add the coconut, apricots, apple, carrots, pecans, and pineapple. Stir to combine.

4. In a separate medium bowl, whisk the eggs. Add the vinegar, sour cream, vanilla, and maple syrup, and whisk until well combined. Pour the wet ingredients into the dry ingredients and stir until combined.

5. Using a ¼ cup measuring cup or ice cream scoop, fill each muffin cup about two-thirds full. Sprinkle raw sugar or coconut sugar on top. Bake for 30 to 35 minutes or until a toothpick inserted into the center comes out clean.

6. Cool in the pan for 5 to 10 minutes, and then transfer to wire rack to cool completely, or serve warm with butter.

Store it

Store in an airtight container at room temperature for up to 3 days or in the freezer for up to 3 months. Thaw at room temperature or reheat in the microwave.

Makes:
1 dozen

Prep time:
20 minutes

Cook time:
30 minutes

These are my favorite muffins! You'll definitely impress your gluten-eating friends with these. They're great for breakfast but also sweet enough for dessert. You can bake this recipe as a coffee cake, but I prefer the muffins because they are easy to grab and go.

Grab 'n' Go Coffee Cake Muffins

1¾ cups #1 All-Purpose Flour Blend (page 24)
1½ tsp xanthan gum
2 tsp baking powder
1 tsp baking soda
½ cup salted butter, softened
½ cup pure cane sugar
½ cup firmly packed light brown sugar
1 cup sour cream
1 tsp apple cider vinegar
1 tsp pure vanilla extract
2 large eggs

Filling
3 tbsp light brown sugar
3 tbsp #1 All-Purpose Flour Blend (page 24)
½ tsp ground cinnamon

Topping
¼ cup firmly packed light brown sugar
¼ cup #1 All-Purpose Flour Blend (page 24)
¼ tsp xanthan gum
¼ tsp ground cinnamon
1½ tbsp salted butter, firm and cut into small pieces

1. Preheat the oven to 350°F (180°C) and line the muffin pans with paper liners. Prepare the cinnamon filling. In a small bowl, stir together the brown sugar, #1 All-Purpose Flour Blend, and cinnamon. Set aside.

2. Prepare the crumb topping. In a small bowl, stir together the brown sugar, #1 All-Purpose Flour Blend, xanthan gum, and cinnamon. Using a pastry cutter or fork, cut in the butter until coarse crumbs are formed. Refrigerate until ready to use.

3. In a small bowl, whisk together the #1 All-Purpose Flour Blend, xanthan gum, baking powder, and baking soda. In a stand mixer fitted with the paddle attachment or in a large bowl, beat the butter, cane sugar, and brown sugar on high speed until well combined. Add the sour cream, vinegar, and vanilla, and beat on high speed for about 2 minutes.

4. Add the eggs one at a time, beating on high speed after each addition. On low speed, slowly beat the flour mixture into the butter mixture until combined.

5. Place 1 tablespoon batter into the bottom of each prepared muffin cup. Top with ½ tablespoon cinnamon filling. Add 2 tablespoons more batter on top of each muffin. (The batter will be thick and you will need to use wet fingers to spread.) Top each muffin with 1 tablespoon crumb topping.

6. Bake for 30 minutes, or until a toothpick inserted into the center comes out clean and the muffin springs back when touched. Cool in the pan for 5 minutes before removing. Serve warm or at room temperature with butter.

Coffee Cake: Grease and lightly flour the bottom of an 8-inch (20cm) square baking pan. Pour half of the batter into the prepared pan. Evenly sprinkle the cinnamon filling on top of the batter. Pour the remaining batter on top of cinnamon filling. Evenly sprinkle the crumb topping mixture on top. Bake for 55 to 60 minutes or until a toothpick inserted into the center comes out clean.

Store it

Store in an airtight container in the refrigerator for up to 5 days or in the freezer for up to 3 months. Thaw at room temperature or reheat in the microwave.

Makes:
16

Prep time:
15 minutes, plus cooling

Cook time:
25 minutes

My mom came to me and said she desperately missed Starbucks's petite vanilla scones after going gluten-free, and she asked me to create a gluten-free version for her. So, here it is. These mini scones taste almost exactly the same!

Petite Vanilla Scones

2 cups #1 All-Purpose Flour Blend (page 24), plus more to flour

2 tsp xanthan gum

4 tbsp pure cane sugar

1 tbsp baking powder

¾ tsp salt

6 tbsp Spectrum palm shortening

2 large eggs

⅓ cup canned coconut cream or heavy whipping cream, plus more to brush

1 tsp pure vanilla extract

1 tsp raw apple cider vinegar

Icing (page 36), to coat

1. Place the rack in the center of the oven and preheat the oven to 400°F (200°C). Line a baking sheet with parchment paper. In a large bowl, whisk together the #1 All-Purpose Flour Blend, xanthan gum, sugar, baking powder, and salt.

2. Using a pastry cutter or fork, cut in the palm shortening until pea-sized crumbs are formed.

3. In a separate medium bowl, lightly whisk the eggs. Then whisk in the coconut cream, vanilla, and vinegar.

4. Make a well in the center of the dry ingredients and pour the cream mixture into the well. Stir carefully until just combined.

5. Turn the dough out onto a piece of parchment paper or lightly floured surface. The dough will be very crumbly and will seem too dry; do not add extra liquid. Gently knead the dough a few times until it is well mixed and sticks together.

6. Form the dough into an 6-inch (15.25cm) square, about 1 to 1¼ inches (2.5–3cm) thick. Dip a knife into some flour, and then cut the dough into four smaller squares. Cut the squares in half diagonally to form 8 triangles. Cut the 8 triangles in half to create 16 mini triangles. Arrange the triangles on the baking sheet.

7. Brush the top of each scone with coconut cream. Bake for 20 to 25 minutes, or until the tops are golden brown. Cool on a wire rack. Once the scones have cooled, dip them in the icing and let dry completely on a wire rack before serving.

Store it

Let the iced scones cool completely. Store in an airtight container on the counter for 1 to 3 days or individually wrapped in the freezer for up to 3 months. Thaw at room temperature or reheat in the oven or microwave.

Tips

This scone is a great base for other flavors. You can add chocolate chips, nuts, or dried fruit, or you can change up the flavor of the icing.

If you need to use another brand of palm shortening, you may find your scones excessively spreading. Chill the dough for at least 1 hour before baking to help prevent the spreading.

Makes:
8

Prep time:
30 minutes

Cook time:
25 minutes

These savory scones are a great alternative to a dinner roll or garlic bread with your meal. The prosciutto and chives punch up the flavor, and the Gruyère gives it a perfect cheesy richness.

Gruyère, Prosciutto & Chive Scones

2 cups #1 All-Purpose Flour Blend (page 24), plus more to flour

2 tsp xanthan gum

2 tbsp pure cane sugar

1 tbsp baking powder

¾ tsp salt

6 tbsp Spectrum palm shortening

½ cup chopped prosciutto

⅔ cup grated Gruyère cheese

¼ cup grated Parmesan cheese

¼ cup chopped chives

3 large eggs, divided

½ cup buttermilk

1 tsp apple cider vinegar

1 tbsp water

1. Preheat the oven to 400°F (200°C) and line a baking sheet with parchment paper. In a large bowl, whisk together the #1 All-Purpose Flour Blend, xanthan gum, sugar, baking powder, and salt.

2. Using a pastry cutter or fork, cut in the palm shortening until pea-sized crumbs are formed. Stir in the prosciutto, Gruyère, Parmesan, and chives.

3. In a separate small bowl, lightly whisk 2 eggs, and then whisk in the buttermilk and vinegar. Make a well in the center of the dry ingredients and pour in the egg–milk mixture. Stir until just combined.

4. Turn the dough out onto a piece of parchment paper or lightly floured surface. The dough will be very crumbly and will seem too dry; do not add extra liquid. Gently knead the dough a few times until it is well mixed and sticks together.

5. Form the dough into a 6-inch (15.25cm) square, about 1¼ inches (3cm) thick. Dip a knife into some flour and then cut the dough into 4 squares. Cut the squares in half diagonally to form 8 triangles. Arrange the triangles on the baking sheet.

6. In a small bowl, whisk together the remaining egg with the water. Brush the egg wash on the scones. Bake for 20 to 25 minutes or until the tops are golden brown. Cool completely on a wire rack before serving.

Store it

Individually wrap in plastic wrap and store in an airtight container in the freezer for up to 3 months. Thaw at room temperature or reheat in the oven.

Tip

If you need to use another brand of palm shortening, you may find your scones excessively spreading. Chill the dough for at least 1 hour before baking to help prevent the spreading.

Makes:
8

Prep time:
15 minutes

Cook time:
25 minutes

These scones will make you feel like royalty enjoying high tea. They have the perfect amount of sweetness with bursts of fresh blueberries and they pair wonderfully with clotted cream and jam. These scones freeze very well and are great to have on hand for a quick breakfast.

Afternoon Tea Blueberry Scones

2 cups plus 1 tbsp #1 All-Purpose Flour Blend (page 24), divided, plus more to flour

2 tsp xanthan gum

3 tbsp pure cane sugar, plus more to top

1 tbsp baking powder

¾ tsp salt

6 tbsp Spectrum palm shortening

1 cup blueberries (fresh, frozen, or dried)

2 large eggs, lightly beaten

⅓ cup canned coconut cream or heavy whipping cream, plus more to brush

1 tsp apple cider vinegar

1. Move the rack to the middle of the oven and preheat the oven to 400°F (200°C). Line a baking sheet with parchment paper. In a large bowl, whisk together 2 cups #1 All-Purpose Flour Blend, xanthan gum, sugar, baking powder, and salt.

2. Using a pastry cutter or fork, cut in the palm shortening until pea-sized crumbs are formed. If using fresh or frozen blueberries, toss them in the remaining 1 tablespoon All-Purpose Flour Blend; this will prevent them from sinking to the bottom. Stir in the blueberries.

3. In a separate medium bowl, lightly whisk the eggs. Then whisk in the coconut cream and vinegar.

4. Make a well in the center of the dry ingredients and pour in the cream mixture. Stir carefully until just combined. The dough will be very crumbly.

5. Turn the dough out onto a piece of parchment paper or lightly floured surface. The dough will be very crumbly and will seem too dry; do not add extra liquid. Gently knead the dough a few times until it is well mixed and sticks together.

6. Form the dough into a 6-inch (15.25cm) square about 1¼ inches (3cm) thick. Dip a knife into some flour and then cut the dough into 4 squares. Cut the squares in half diagonally to form 8 triangles. Arrange the triangles on the baking sheet.

7. Brush the tops of each scone with coconut cream and sprinkle with sugar. Bake for 20 to 25 minutes or until the tops are golden brown. Cool on a wire rack before serving.

Store it

Store in an airtight container on the counter for 2 to 3 days, refrigerate for up to 5 days, or freeze, individually wrapped, for up to 3 months. Thaw at room temperature or reheat in the microwave.

Tip

If you need to use another brand of palm shortening, you may find your scones excessively spreading. Chill the dough for at least 1 hour before baking to help prevent the spreading.

Makes:
8

Prep time:
25 minutes, plus cooling

Cook time:
25 minutes

Have you ever had a maple scone from Starbucks? They are pretty incredible. I used to get so excited every fall when they would start carrying them. I have not had a Starbucks scone in a very long time, but these scones bring me right back to the days of maple scones and lattes on my way to work.

Coffee Shop Maple Scones

2 cups #1 All-Purpose Flour Blend (page 24)

2 tsp xanthan gum

2 tbsp pure cane sugar

1 tbsp baking powder

¾ tsp salt

6 tbsp Spectrum palm shortening

½ cup chopped pecans

2 large eggs

⅓ cup heavy whipping cream

2 tbsp pure maple syrup

1 tsp apple cider vinegar

Maple Icing

2 cups powdered sugar

¼ cup pure maple syrup

½–1 tbsp whole milk

1. Preheat the oven to 400°F (200°C) and line a baking sheet with parchment paper. In a large bowl, whisk together the #1 All-Purpose Flour Blend, xanthan gum, sugar, baking powder, and salt.

2. Using a pastry cutter or fork, cut in the palm shortening until pea-sized crumbs are formed. Stir in the pecans.

3. In a separate medium bowl, lightly whisk the eggs. Then whisk in the cream, maple syrup, and vinegar.

4. Make a well in the center of the dry ingredients and pour in the cream mixture. Stir carefully until just combined.

5. Turn the dough out onto a piece of parchment paper or lightly floured surface. The dough will be very crumbly and will seem too dry; do not add extra liquid. Gently knead the dough a few times until it is well mixed and sticks together.

6. Form the dough into a 6-inch (15.25cm) square about 1¼ inches (3cm) thick. Dip a knife into some flour and then cut the dough into 4 squares. Cut the squares in half diagonally to form 8 triangles. Arrange the triangles on the baking sheet.

7. Bake for 20 to 25 minutes or until the tops are golden brown. Cool on a wire rack. Dip the cooled scones in the icing, and let set on the wire racks before serving.

   Maple Icing: In a small bowl, stir together the powdered sugar, maple syrup, and ½ tablespoon milk. Add more milk 1 teaspoon at a time until a smooth, thin icing is formed.

Store it

Let the iced scones cool completely. Store in an airtight container on the counter for 1 to 3 days or individually wrapped in the freezer for up to 3 months. Thaw at room temperature or reheat in the oven or microwave.

Tip

If you need to use another brand of palm shortening, you may find your scones excessively spreading. Chill the dough for at least 1 hour before baking to help prevent the spreading.

Pies & Fruity Desserts

Buttery Pie Crust.................................138

Mom's Apple Pie.................................139

Holiday Pecan Pie.............................140

Pumpkin Pie..142

Fresh Strawberry Pie......................143

Peach Cobbler....................................145

Mock Cherry Cheesecake..................146

Apple Crisp...147

Pear Tart...148

Makes:
2 (9-in/23cm) crusts

Prep time:
15 minutes, plus
2 hours to chill

Cook time:
None

Sometimes the best part of pie is the buttery, flaky crust. But let's face it, store-bought pie crusts are anything but buttery, flaky, and tasty, and I'm not even talking about the gluten-free ones, which are nonexistent in the average store. This is a great multipurpose crust for sweet pies, quiches, pot pies, or any recipe calling for a pie crust.

Buttery Pie Crust

2¼ cups #1 All-Purpose Flour Blend (page 24)

1 tsp xanthan gum

2 tbsp pure cane sugar (optional; omit for savory recipes)

¾ cup salted butter, firm and cut into ¼-in (0.5cm) pieces

5–7 tbsp ice-cold water

1. In a food processor, add the #1 All-Purpose Flour Blend, xanthan gum, and sugar (if using). Pulse until combined. Add the butter and pulse until the mixture resembles a coarse meal.

2. Add the ice-cold water 1 tablespoon at a time, pulsing to combine after each addition. The dough should hold together when squeezed but not be too sticky.

3. Divide and shape the dough into two even disks. Wrap each half separately in plastic wrap and refrigerate for at least 2 hours, or up to 2 days. (The dough can be frozen at this point, too, and used within 3 months.)

4. Before baking, remove the disk(s) from the refrigerator and let sit at room temperature for 5 to 10 minutes. Place the disk between two sheets of parchment paper, on a silicone baking mat, or between two pieces of floured plastic wrap. Roll out the dough into a 12-inch (30.5cm) round crust, about ¹⁄₁₆ to ⅛ inches (1.5–3mm) thick. If the dough begins to stick to the surface, lightly flour the work surface and the top of dough.

5. Either blind bake your crust (see below), or proceed with your recipe using the unbaked rolled-out crust.

   Blind Bake: Mold the bottom crust into a pie pan and freeze for 30 minutes. (Leave the top crust in the refrigerator, if using.) Position the oven rack in the lower third of the oven. Place a baking sheet on the rack and preheat the sheet and the oven to 400°F. In a small bowl, whisk together 1 egg and 1 tablespoon water. Brush the edge of the pie crust with the egg wash. Line the bottom of the crust with parchment paper and pie weights and bake for 20 minutes. Remove the parchment and bake for 5 minutes more.

Tip ....

Make extra pie crust dough and store the disks in the freezer. That way you have pie crust available anytime you feel like making a Chicken Pot Pie (page 57).

Makes:
1 (9-in/23cm) pie

Prep time:
30 minutes

Cook time:
1 hour

My mom has always made the most amazing apple pie with a crumb topping. It was a staple of our Thanksgiving dinner, and I would always save room for it. I think my favorite part was having a slice for breakfast the next morning! This recipe is the gluten-free version of my mom's recipe.

Mom's Apple Pie

1 unbaked Buttery Pie Crust (page 138)
Vanilla ice cream, to serve

Topping
1½ cups #1 All-Purpose Flour Blend (page 24)
1 tsp xanthan gum
¾ cup firmly packed light brown sugar
½ tsp ground cinnamon
¾ cup salted butter, firm and cut into small pieces

Filling
1 cup pure cane sugar
¼ cup #1 All-Purpose Flour Blend (page 24)
½ tsp xanthan gum
Pinch of ground nutmeg
2 tsp ground cinnamon
Dash of salt
8–10 cups peeled and sliced tart apples (such as Granny Smith; 6–8 whole apples)

1. Mold the unbaked pie crust into a 9-inch (23cm) deep-dish pie pan and freeze for 30 minutes.

2. Preheat the oven to 425°F (220°C). Prepare the topping. In a small bowl, stir together the #1 All-Purpose Flour Blend, xanthan gum, brown sugar, and cinnamon until combined. Using a fork or your hands, cut in the cold butter until the butter is well disbursed and pea-sized crumbs are formed. Set aside.

3. Prepare the filling. In a large bowl, stir together the sugar, #1 All-Purpose Flour Blend, xanthan gum, nutmeg, cinnamon, and salt. Stir in the apples until well coated.

4. Pour the apples into the prepared pie crust (mounded high). Evenly spoon the topping over the apples. Carefully spread the topping over the apples until they are all covered, and press down lightly.

5. Bake for 50 to 60 minutes or until golden brown and the apples are soft when pierced with a fork. Cover the pie with foil for the last 20 to 25 minutes if the topping starts to get too brown.

6. Cool on a wire rack. Serve warm or at room temperature alongside vanilla ice cream.

Store it

Cover with plastic wrap or transfer to an airtight container and refrigerate for up to 3 days.

Makes:
1 (9-in/23cm) pie

Prep time:
45 minutes

Cook time:
1 hour 10 minutes

Pecan is usually my pie of choice, and this version satisfies. It's incredibly sweet, chewy and delicious, and pairs perfectly with vanilla ice cream! When I was selling my baked goods to local stores, I made this pie during the holidays. It was a huge hit and so easy to make.

Holiday Pecan Pie

1 unbaked Buttery Pie Crust (page 138)

1 cup pure cane sugar

3 tbsp light brown sugar

½ tsp salt

1 cup light corn syrup

⅓ cup salted butter, melted and cooled

1 tsp pure vanilla extract

3 large eggs

1¼ cup chopped pecans

1. Mold the rolled-out pie crust into a 9-inch (23cm) deep-dish pie pan and freeze for 30 minutes. While the pie crust is freezing, preheat the oven to 350°F (180°C).

2. In a medium bowl, whisk together the cane sugar, brown sugar, salt, corn syrup, melted butter, vanilla, and eggs until well combined.

3. Remove the pie crust from the freezer and spread the chopped pecans in the bottom of the uncooked crust. Pour the sugar mixture over the pecans.

4. Lightly cover the pie with foil without letting the foil touch the pie mixture and bake for 40 minutes. Remove the foil and bake for 20 to 30 minutes more, or until the filling is set. Let cool completely before cutting. Serve at room temperature.

Store it

Cover with plastic wrap or transfer to an airtight container and refrigerate for up to 5 days.

Makes:
1 (9-in/23cm) pie

Prep time:
10 minutes, plus
2 hours to chill

Cook time:
1 hour 5 minutes

Some holidays are not complete unless you smell pumpkin pie baking in the oven. This is a great pie to make for your gluten-eating friends—with the naturally gluten-free filling and the flaky crust, it's just as good as any other version out there.

Pumpkin Pie

1 unbaked Buttery Pie Crust
   (page 138)
¾ cup pure cane sugar
½ tsp salt
1 tsp ground cinnamon
¼ tsp ground ginger
¼ tsp ground nutmeg
⅛ tsp ground cloves
2 large eggs
1 (15oz/420g) can 100% pure
   pumpkin
1 (12fl oz/350ml) can evaporated
   milk

1. Preheat the oven to 425°F (220°C) and mold the unbaked pie crust into a 9-inch (23cm) deep-dish pie pan.

2. In a small bowl, mix together the sugar, salt, cinnamon, ginger, nutmeg, and cloves.

3. In a stand mixer fitted with the paddle attachment or in a large bowl, beat the eggs on high speed. Stir in the pumpkin and sugar mixture. Gradually whisk in the evaporated milk.

4. Pour the filling into the prepared pie crust. Bake for 15 minutes and then reduce the oven temperature to 350°F (180°C). Continue to bake for another 40 to 50 minutes or until a knife inserted near the center comes out clean. If the edges of the pie crust start to get too dark, cover the edges with foil.

5. Cool on a wire rack for 2 hours and then store in the refrigerator. Serve cold or at room temperature.

Store it

Cover with plastic wrap or transfer to an airtight container and refrigerate for up to 5 days.

Makes:
1 (9-in/23cm) pie

Prep time:
20 minutes, plus 5 hours
for the crust and to chill

Cook time:
10 minutes

Growing up in California where Marie Callender's restaurants were prevalent, we would often purchase their pies for special occasions. The fresh strawberry pie was always my favorite (and my brother's). Now when strawberry season rolls around, I make my own version of the pie. It's best served within 6 hours of making it.

Fresh Strawberry Pie

1 blind baked Buttery Pie Crust
   (page 138)
4lb (2kg) fresh strawberries,
   hulled, divided
¾ cup pure cane sugar
1½ tbsp cornstarch
1½ tsp unflavored gelatin
Pinch of salt
1 tbsp fresh lemon juice

Whipped Cream Topping
1 cup heavy whipping cream
4 tbsp powdered sugar
1 tsp pure vanilla extract
1 tsp unflavored gelatin
1 tbsp water

1. Mold the pie crust into a 9-inch (23cm) deep-dish pie pan and follow the instructions on page 138 to blind bake the crust. Completely cool before filling.

2. Chop 1½ cups of strawberries, leaving the rest whole. In a food processor or blender, process the 1½ cups chopped strawberries into a smooth purée. (You should have about ¾ cup purée.)

3. In a medium saucepan over medium-high heat, whisk together the strawberry purée, sugar, cornstarch, gelatin, and salt until well combined. Continue cooking and stirring constantly until the mixture comes to a full boil. Boil for 2 minutes, constantly stirring and scraping the bottom and sides of the pan to prevent burning. After boiling for 2 minutes, pour the mixture into a large bowl.

4. Whisk in the lemon juice. Let the glaze cool to room temperature.

5. Cut any of the extra-large strawberries in half. Gently fold all of the remaining strawberries into the cooled glaze until the strawberries are well coated.

6. Spoon the strawberries into the cooled pie crust and pile into a large mound. Refrigerate for 2 hours. Using a pastry bag with a large icing tip, pipe the whipped cream topping onto the chilled pie or dollop on each individual slice before serving.

Whipped Cream Topping:

1. In the bowl of a stand mixer or in a large metal bowl, stir together the cream, powdered sugar, and vanilla. Refrigerate the bowl along with the whisk attachment for 5 minutes.

2. While the mixture is chilling, in a small microwave-safe bowl, combine the gelatin with the water. When the gelatin has completely absorbed the water, microwave the mixture for 15 seconds to liquefy. Stir and let sit until it reaches room temperature.

3. Remove the bowl from the refrigerator. Using the chilled whisk attachment, beat the cream mixture on medium-high speed until soft peaks form. Slowly drizzle in the liquid gelatin mixture. (If the gelatin has hardened back up, microwave for a few seconds until liquid again, but be sure it cools a bit before adding.) Beat until stiff peaks form. Refrigerate until ready to use.

Store it

This pie is best eaten the day it's made. To store, cover with plastic wrap and refrigerate for 1 to 2 days.

During peach season, we make this cobbler over and over again in my house. Served slightly warm with a scoop of vanilla ice cream is my favorite way to eat it. This gluten-free version tastes just as good for breakfast the next morning.

Peach Cobbler

Vanilla ice cream, to serve

Filling

5 cups sliced fresh peaches
(8–10 small peaches or
5–6 large peaches)
1 tsp fresh lemon juice
⅓ cup pure cane sugar
1 tbsp cornstarch
¼ tsp ground cinnamon
¼ cup water

Topping

1¼ cups #1 All-Purpose Flour
Blend (page 24)
⅛ tsp xanthan gum
⅓ cup pure cane sugar
½ tsp salt
1 tbsp baking powder
4 tbsp salted butter, melted
and cooled
2 tsp pure vanilla extract
1 tsp apple cider vinegar
¾ cup whole milk
Turbinado sugar, to sprinkle

1. Preheat the oven to 375°F (190°C) and prepare the peach filling. In a medium saucepan, stir together the peaches, lemon juice, sugar, cornstarch, cinnamon, and water over medium-high heat. Bring to a boil and cook until the peaches start to soften and the liquid is slightly thick, 8 to 10 minutes. Pour the peach mixture into a 2-quart (2 liter) baking dish.

2. Prepare the topping. In a medium bowl, whisk together the #1 All-Purpose Flour Blend, xanthan gum, sugar, salt, and baking powder.

3. In a separate medium bowl, whisk together the melted butter, vanilla, vinegar, and milk until well combined.

4. Pour the wet ingredients into the flour mixture and stir until well combined. Let sit for 2 to 3 minutes to slightly thicken up. Arrange the topping over the peach mixture. Sprinkle with turbinado sugar.

5. Bake for 30 to 35 minutes or until the peaches are very soft, the topping is golden brown, and a toothpick inserted into the topping comes out clean. Serve warm or at room temperature alongside a scoop of vanilla ice cream.

Store it

Store in an airtight container in the refrigerator for up to 5 days. Eat leftovers cold, at room temperature, or slightly warmed up in the microwave or oven.

Tip

If it's not peach season, you can substitute frozen sliced peaches for the fresh peaches. Thaw the peaches before using.

Makes:
1 (9 x 13-in/23 x 33cm) cheesecake

Prep time:
30 minutes, plus 2 hours to chill

Cook time:
15 minutes

Growing up, we served this cheesecake at most parties, and it was always a fan favorite. Cheesecakes can sometimes be tricky to make, but with this foolproof recipe, it'll seem like you spent hours preparing it. The sweet, creamy cheese layer combined with the tart cherries is the perfect combination.

Mock Cherry Cheesecake

2 (21oz/595g) cans cherry pie filling

Crust
1 cup salted butter, softened
2 cups #1 All-Purpose Flour Blend (page 24)
½ cup firmly packed light brown sugar
1 tsp xanthan gum
1 cup finely chopped pecans or walnuts

Filling
8oz (225g) cream cheese, room temperature
1 cup powdered sugar
1 tsp pure vanilla extract
12oz (340g) frozen whipped topping (such as Cool Whip), thawed

1. Preheat the oven to 350°F (180°C). Make the crust. In a large bowl, add the butter, #1 All-Purpose Flour Blend, brown sugar, xanthan gum, and pecans. Using your hands, mix the ingredients together until well combined.

2. Pour the crust mixture into a 9 x 13-inch (23 x 33cm) baking dish, and press evenly into the pan. Bake for 15 minutes. Let cool completely.

3. Prepare the filling. In a stand mixer fitted with the paddle attachment or in a large bowl, add the cream cheese, powdered sugar, vanilla, and whipped topping. Beat on medium-high speed until well combined and smooth.

4. When the crust is cooled, spread the filling evenly over the crust. Spread the cherry pie filling evenly over the top. Chill in the refrigerator for 2 hours. Cut into squares and serve.

Store it
Cover with plastic wrap and refrigerate for up to 5 days.

Tip
Substitute strawberry or blueberry pie filling for the cherry pie filling, if desired.

Serves:
9–12

Prep time:
20 minutes

Cook time:
40 minutes

In my opinion, the topping is always the best part of any type of crisp. When creating this recipe, I made sure that every bite of apple had an ample amount of crispy, sweet topping. Because the ingredients are simple staples, it's a great last-minute recipe!

Apple Crisp

5 medium Granny Smith apples, peeled and chopped (roughly ½-in/1.25cm pieces)

1⅛ cups firmly packed light brown sugar

¾ cup #1 All-Purpose Flour Blend (page 24)

¾ cup old-fashioned rolled oats (certified gluten-free)

1 tsp ground cinnamon

1 tsp xanthan gum

½ tsp ground nutmeg

½ cup salted butter, cut into cubes and slightly softened

Vanilla ice cream or whipped cream (optional), to serve

1. Preheat the oven to 375°F (190°C). Spread the peeled and chopped apples in the bottom of an 8- or 9-inch (20 or 23cm) square deep-dish pan.

2. In a medium bowl, stir together the brown sugar, #1 All-Purpose Flour Blend, oats, cinnamon, xanthan gum, and nutmeg until well combined.

3. Using a pastry cutter or your hands, cut in the butter until pea-sized crumbs are formed.

4. Evenly sprinkle the topping over the apples. Bake for 35 to 40 minutes or until the topping is golden brown and the apples are soft when pierced with a fork.

5. Let cool for at least 10 minutes before serving. Serve warm by itself, or topped with vanilla ice cream or whipped cream.

Store it

Cover with plastic wrap and refrigerate for up to 3 days. Enjoy chilled, at room temperature, or slightly rewarmed in the oven or microwave (my favorite).

Makes:
1 (9-in/23cm) tart

Prep time:
4 hours

Cook time:
30 minutes

This dessert is sure to impress your friends. It's so easy to make and yet so beautiful with the arrangement of pears on top. The sweetness of the glaze and pears is perfect with the cream cheese filling. A scoop of vanilla ice cream is amazing to top it off.

Pear Tart

1 unbaked Buttery Pie Crust
  (page 138)
4 pears
1 tsp fresh lemon juice
8oz (225g) cream cheese,
  softened
¼ cup pure cane sugar
1 large egg
1 tsp pure vanilla extract

Glaze
¼ cup apricot jam
½ tsp pure vanilla extract
½ tsp fresh lemon juice
2 tbsp water

1. Mold the pie crust into a 9-inch (23cm) tart pan, pressing the crust into the fluted sides, and freeze for 30 minutes. While the crust is freezing, preheat the oven to 375°F (190°C).

2. Once the crust is frozen, place a round piece of parchment paper in the bottom of the crust and fill with pie weights. Bake for 10 minutes.

3. While the crust is baking, prepare the pears and filling. Peel and thinly slice the pears (about ¼-in/0.5cm thick) and toss with the lemon juice. Set aside.

4. After baking the crust, increase the oven temperature to 425°F (220°C). In a stand mixer fitted with the paddle attachment or in a medium bowl, beat the cream cheese and sugar on high speed until smooth. Beat in the egg and vanilla until combined.

5. Spread the filling into the par-baked crust. Arrange the pears on top of the filling in a circular pattern.

6. Bake the tart for 10 minutes. Lower the heat to 350°F (180°C) and continue baking for 15 to 20 minutes, or until the filling is set.

7. While the tart is baking, prepare the glaze. In a small saucepan, cook the apricot jam, vanilla, lemon juice, and water over medium heat for 6 to 8 minutes or until melted and smooth. Strain out the solids, if desired.

8. Brush the glaze onto the pears of the cooked tart. Broil the tart for 1 to 2 minutes or until shiny, being careful not to let it burn.

9. Cool the tart on a wire rack for 1 hour. Transfer the tart to the refrigerator and chill for at least 2 hours before serving. Serve cold.

Store it

Store in an airtight container in the refrigerator for up to 5 days.

Cakes & Cupcakes

Chocolate Cupcakes 152

Vanilla Cupcakes 153

Strawberry Shortcake Cupcakes 154

Lemon Cupcakes with
Raspberry Buttercream 156

Black Forest Cupcakes 157

Lemon Pound Cake 159

Rex's Favorite Pumpkin
Cupcakes 160

Super Moist Pineapple
Carrot Cake 161

Glazed Triple Chocolate
Bundt Cake 162

Red Velvet Cake 164

Boston Cream Pie 165

County Fair Funnel Cakes 167

Sending your gluten-free child to a party is always a bit tricky, especially when it's time for cake. I never wanted my children to miss out, so I made a chocolate cupcake that was equally good (if not better) than the gluten-filled cupcakes being served. Mission accomplished! You can also use this recipe to make a cake.

Chocolate Cupcakes

2 cups pure cane sugar

1 cup salted butter, softened

3 large eggs, room temperature

2½ cups #1 All-Purpose Flour Blend (page 24)

½ tsp salt

1½ tsp baking powder

½ tsp baking soda

1 cup cocoa powder

2 tsp xanthan gum

½ cup brewed coffee (hot or cold)

1 cup whole milk

2 tsp pure vanilla extract

2 tsp apple cider vinegar

Chocolate Buttercream Frosting

1½ cups salted butter, softened

1 cup cocoa powder

5–6 cups powdered sugar, divided

6–8 tbsp heavy whipping cream

1 tsp pure vanilla extract

1. Preheat the oven to 350°F (180°C) and line the muffin pans with paper liners. In a stand mixer fitted with the paddle attachment or in a large bowl, cream the sugar and butter on medium-high speed until light and fluffy, 3 to 5 minutes.

2. Beat in eggs one at a time until incorporated. In a separate medium bowl, sift together the #1 All-Purpose Flour Blend, salt, baking powder, baking soda, cocoa powder, and xanthan gum.

3. Slowly beat the dry ingredients into the butter mixture on low speed until combined. While on low speed, slowly add the coffee, milk, vanilla, and vinegar, and beat until well combined.

4. Using a ¼ cup measuring cup or ice cream scoop, fill each muffin cup about two-thirds full. Bake for 20 to 25 minutes or until the cupcakes spring back when touched and a toothpick inserted into the center comes out clean.

5. Cool in the pan for 3 minutes and then transfer to a wire rack to cool completely. Once completely cooled, frost the cupcakes.

Chocolate Buttercream Frosting: In a stand mixer fitted with the paddle attachment or in a large bowl, beat the butter for 1 minute on high speed. On low speed, slowly add the cocoa powder and beat until well combined. Add 2½ cups powdered sugar. Increase the speed to high and beat for 2 minutes. Then add 6 tablespoons cream, vanilla, and 2½ cups more powdered sugar. Beat on low speed to incorporate, and then increase the speed to high and beat for 3 to 5 minutes. Beat in more sugar or cream as needed to reach the desired consistency.

Chocolate Cake: Grease and lightly flour only the bottoms of two (9-in/23cm) round cake pans. Portion equal amounts of batter into each cake pan, gently tapping them on the counter to evenly spread. Bake for 40 to 45 minutes or until a toothpick inserted into the center comes out clean. Let cool in the pans on a wire rack for 10 minutes. Remove from the pans and cool completely on wire racks. Frost once completely cooled.

Store it

Store the frosted cupcakes in an airtight container in the refrigerator for up to 1 day or in the freezer for up to 3 months. Thaw at room temperature.

Makes:
2 dozen

Prep time:
30 minutes, plus cooling

Cook time:
25 minutes

If you're either chocolate or vanilla, then I'm definitely vanilla. A fluffy white cake with buttercream frosting has always been my favorite. This recipe took many attempts to create but was so worth the effort. Whenever I serve these cupcakes to family and friends, they're shocked they're gluten-free because they're so moist and light.

Vanilla Cupcakes

2 cups pure cane sugar

1 cup salted butter, room temperature

4 large eggs, separated

2 tsp pure vanilla extract

3 cups #2 All-Purpose Flour Blend (page 24)

1½ tsp xanthan gum

1 tbsp baking powder

2 tsp apple cider vinegar

1 cup whole milk

Buttercream Frosting

1½ cups salted butter, softened

6–7 cups powdered sugar, divided

6–8 tbsp heavy whipping cream

1½ tsp pure vanilla extract

1. Preheat the oven to 350°F (180°C) and line the muffin pans with paper liners. In a stand mixer fitted with the paddle attachment or in a large bowl, cream the sugar and butter on medium-high speed until light and fluffy, 3 to 5 minutes.

2. Beat in the egg yolks one at a time until incorporated. In a separate medium bowl, combine the #2 All-Purpose Flour Blend, xanthan gum, and baking powder. Add to the butter mixture and mix well on low speed.

3. In a separate small bowl, beat the egg whites on high speed until stiff peaks form.

4. On low speed, mix the milk and vinegar into the cake batter. Gently fold the egg whites into the batter.

5. Using a ¼ cup measuring cup or ice cream scoop, fill each muffin cup about two-thirds full. Bake for 20 to 25 minutes or until the cupcakes spring back when touched and a toothpick inserted into the center comes out clean.

6. Cool in the pan for 5 minutes and then transfer to a wire rack to cool completely. Once completely cooled, frost the cupcakes.

Buttercream Frosting: In a stand mixer fitted with the paddle attachment or in a large bowl, beat the butter for 1 minute on high speed. On low speed, slowly add 3 cups powdered sugar. Increase the speed to high and beat for 2 minutes. Then add 6 tablespoons cream, vanilla, and 3 cups more powdered sugar. Beat on low speed to incorporate, and then increase the speed to high and beat for 3 to 5 minutes. Beat in more sugar or cream as needed to reach the desired consistency.

Store it

Store the frosted cupcakes in an airtight container in the refrigerator for up to 2 days or in the freezer for up to 3 months. Thaw at room temperature.

Tips

Use a piping bag and a large icing tip for the prettiest result! My favorite tip is a Wilton 1M open star icing tip.

I like to keep a few of these in the freezer at all times so I'm always prepared for when my kids are invited to a party. I can send them to the party with a cupcake in a small airtight container, and then they are not left out at cake time.

Makes:
2 dozen

Prep time:
30 minutes, plus cooling

Cook time:
25 minutes

These cupcakes are a variation of strawberry shortcake conveniently made into a cupcake. The whipped cream frosting is also much lighter than buttercream frosting, creating a lighter dessert than my vanilla cupcake. Sometimes I place a blueberry on top and serve them for the Fourth of July!

Strawberry Shortcake Cupcakes

2 cups pure cane sugar

1 cup salted butter, softened

4 large eggs, separated

3 tsp pure vanilla extract

3 cups #2 All-Purpose Flour Blend (page 24)

1½ tsp xanthan gum

3 tsp baking powder

1 cup whole milk

1 tsp apple cider vinegar

Filling

16oz (450g) strawberries, coarsely chopped

1 cup heavy whipping cream

⅓ cup powdered sugar, plus more to dust

1. Preheat the oven to 350°F (180°C) and line the muffin pans with paper liners. In a stand mixer fitted with the paddle attachment or in a large bowl, cream the sugar and butter on medium-high speed until light and fluffy, 3 to 5 minutes.

2. Beat in the egg yolks and vanilla until combined. In a medium bowl, whisk together the #2 All-Purpose Flour Blend, xanthan gum, and baking powder. Add the dry mixture to the wet mixture and mix well on low speed. Stir in the milk and vinegar.

3. In a separate medium bowl, beat the egg whites on high speed until soft peaks form. Gently fold the egg whites into the batter.

4. Using a ¼ cup measuring cup or ice cream scoop, fill each muffin cup about two-thirds full. Bake for 20 to 25 minutes or until the cupcakes spring back when touched and a toothpick inserted into the center comes out clean. Cool in the pan for 5 minutes, and then transfer to a wire rack to cool completely.

5. While the cupcakes are cooling, make the filling. In a medium bowl, use a fork or potato masher to mash the chopped strawberries. In a stand mixer fitted with the whisk attachment or in a separate medium bowl, beat the cream and powdered sugar until stiff peaks form. Drain the strawberries and then fold the mashed strawberries into the whipped cream.

6. Assemble the cupcakes. Carefully remove the paper liner from each cupcake and cut the top off of each. Spoon about 2 tablespoons of the strawberry cream mixture atop each cupcake bottom. Place the cupcake tops back on top of the cupcakes. Dust the tops with powdered sugar. Serve immediately.

Store it

Cover the assembled cupcakes with plastic wrap and refrigerate for up to 2 days. I do not recommend freezing these cupcakes because of the delicate filling.

Tip

You can make both the cupcakes and the filling up to 1 day in advance and store in separate airtight containers in the refrigerator. Assemble the cupcakes right before serving.

Makes:
2 dozen

Prep time:
20 minutes, plus cooling

Cook time:
25 minutes

Looking to change things up from a plain vanilla cupcake? These would be a great choice. The raspberry buttercream frosting makes them so pretty and complements the lemon flavor perfectly.

Lemon Cupcakes
with Raspberry Buttercream

2 cups pure cane sugar

1 cup salted butter, softened

4 large eggs, separated

Zest of 1 lemon

2 tbsp fresh lemon juice

3 cups #2 All-Purpose Flour Blend (page 24)

1½ tsp xanthan gum

1 tbsp baking powder

2 tsp apple cider vinegar

1 cup whole milk

Raspberry Buttercream Frosting

6oz (170g) fresh raspberries

1½ cups salted butter, softened

6–7 cups powdered sugar, divided

6–8 tbsp heavy whipping cream

1½ tsp pure vanilla extract

1. Preheat the oven to 350°F (180°C) and line the muffin pans with paper liners. In a stand mixer fitted with the paddle attachment or in a large bowl, cream the sugar and butter on medium-high speed until light and fluffy, 3 to 5 minutes.

2. Beat in the egg yolks, lemon zest, and lemon juice on medium-high speed until well combined.

3. In a separate medium bowl, whisk together the #2 All-Purpose Flour Blend, xanthan gum, and baking powder. Add the dry mixture to the wet mixture and mix well on low speed.

4. In a separate medium bowl, beat the egg whites until stiff peaks form.

5. On low speed, mix the vinegar and milk into the cake batter. Gently fold the egg whites into the batter.

6. Using a ¼ cup measuring cup or ice cream scoop, fill each muffin cup about two-thirds full. Bake for 20 to 25 minutes or until the cupcakes spring back when touched and a toothpick inserted into the center comes out clean.

7. Cool in the pan for 5 minutes and then transfer to a wire rack to cool completely. Once completely cooled, frost the cupcakes.

Raspberry Buttercream Frosting: In a blender or food processor, purée the raspberries and then pour through a fine mesh sieve, discarding the solids. In a stand mixer fitted with the paddle attachment or in a large bowl, beat the butter for 1 minute on high speed. On low speed, slowly add 3 cups powdered sugar. Increase the speed to high and beat for 2 minutes. Add the raspberry purée, 6 tablespoons cream, vanilla, and 3 cups more powdered sugar. Beat on low speed to incorporate, and then increase the speed to high and beat for 3 to 5 minutes. Beat in more sugar or cream as needed to reach the desired consistency.

Store it

Store the frosted cupcakes in an airtight container in the refrigerator for up to 1 day or in the freezer for up to 3 months. Thaw at room temperature.

Tip

Use a piping bag and a large icing tip for the prettiest result. My favorite tip is a Wilton 1M open star icing tip.

Makes:
2 dozen

Prep time:
50 minutes, plus cooling

Cook time:
25 minutes

With brewed coffee and cherry pie filling, I think of these cupcakes as the grown-up version of a standard chocolate cupcake. They're so pretty with chocolate shavings and a cherry on top, and the whipped cream frosting is light and yummy.

Black Forest Cupcakes

2 cups pure cane sugar

1 cup salted butter, softened

3 large eggs, room temperature

2½ cups #1 All-Purpose Flour Blend (page 24)

½ tsp salt

1½ tsp baking powder

½ tsp baking soda

1 cup cocoa powder

2 tsp xanthan gum

½ cup brewed coffee (hot or cold)

1 cup whole milk

2 tsp pure vanilla extract

2 tsp apple cider vinegar

1 (21oz/595g) can cherry pie filling

Milk or dark chocolate bar, finely grated, to decorate

24 maraschino cherries or fresh cherries with stems

Whipped Cream Frosting

1½ tsp unflavored gelatin

2 tbsp water

1½ cups heavy whipping cream

⅓ cup powdered sugar

1 tsp pure vanilla extract

1. Preheat the oven to 350°F (180°C) and line the muffin pans with paper liners. In a stand mixer fitted with the paddle attachment or in a large bowl, cream the sugar and butter on medium-high speed until light and fluffy, 3 to 5 minutes.

2. Beat in the eggs one at a time until incorporated. In a separate medium bowl, whisk together the #1 All-Purpose Flour Blend, salt, baking powder, baking soda, cocoa powder, and xanthan gum. On low speed, beat the dry ingredients into the wet mixture until combined.

3. On low speed, slowly add the coffee, milk, vanilla, and vinegar. Increase the speed to medium and beat until well combined, scraping down the sides of the bowl as needed. Let the batter rest for 5 minutes.

4. Using a ¼ cup measuring cup or large ice cream scoop, fill each muffin cup about two-thirds full. Bake for 20 to 25 minutes or until the cupcakes spring back when touched and a toothpick inserted into the center comes out clean.

5. Cool in the pan for 5 minutes and then transfer to a wire rack to cool completely. Once completely cooled, cut out a small cone-shaped hole in the middle of each cupcake, discarding the removed portion. Fill each hole with cherry pie filling. Using an icing bag with a large icing tip, pipe on the whipped cream frosting. Top with chocolate shavings and a cherry. Refrigerate until ready to serve.

Whipped Cream Frosting: In a small microwave-safe bowl, combine the gelatin with the water. When the gelatin has completely absorbed the water, microwave the mixture for 15 seconds to liquefy. Stir and let sit until it reaches room temperature. In the bowl of a stand mixer fitted with the whisk attachment or in a large bowl, beat the cream, powdered sugar, and vanilla on medium-high speed. As it starts to thicken, slowly drizzle in the liquid gelatin mixture. (If the gelatin has hardened back up, microwave for a few seconds until liquid again, but be sure it cools a bit before adding.) Beat until stiff peaks form. Refrigerate until ready to use.

Store it

Store in an airtight container in the refrigerator for up to 2 days. I do not recommend freezing these cupcakes because of the delicate frosting.

Serves:
1 (9 x 5-in/23 x 12.5cm) loaf

Prep time:
15 minutes, plus cooling

Cook time:
55 minutes

This pound cake is amazing with fresh strawberries or raspberries piled on top with powdered sugar or whipped cream—one of my all-time favorite desserts. I created this loaf to add to the selection of loaves I was selling, and it became very popular, especially during strawberry season.

Lemon Pound Cake

1½ cups pure cane sugar
¾ cup salted butter, softened
3 large eggs
2 tbsp fresh lemon juice
Zest of 1 lemon
1 tsp pure vanilla extract
2 cups #1 All-Purpose Flour Blend (page 24)
1 tsp baking powder
½ tsp baking soda
½ tsp salt
2 tsp xanthan gum
½ cup sour cream
Fresh raspberries or strawberry slices, whipped cream, and powdered sugar (optional), to serve

Glaze
1 cup powdered sugar
1 tbsp fresh lemon juice
2 tsp light vegetable oil (such as avocado oil)
2 tsp water

1. Place the oven rack at the lower third of the oven and preheat the oven to 350°F (180°C). Lightly grease only the bottom of a 9 x 5-inch (23 x 12.5cm) loaf pan.

2. In a stand mixer fitted with the paddle attachment or in a large bowl, cream the sugar and butter, starting on low speed and gradually increasing to high speed, until light and fluffy, 3 to 5 minutes.

3. Beat in the eggs one at a time until incorporated. Beat in the lemon juice, lemon zest, and vanilla until fully incorporated.

4. In a separate medium bowl, whisk together the #1 All-Purpose Flour Blend, baking powder, baking soda, salt, and xanthan gum.

5. On low speed, alternate adding the flour mixture with the sour cream into the butter-sugar mixture. Beat until combined.

6. Pour the batter into the loaf pan and bake for 50 to 55 minutes or until a toothpick inserted into the center comes out clean. Cool completely in the pan. Once cooled, gently turn out of the pan.

7. Drizzle the glaze over the cooled cake. Slice and serve at room temperature with strawberries or raspberries, whipped cream, and a sprinkle of powdered sugar (if using).

   Glaze: In a small bowl, whisk all of the ingredients together until smooth.

Store it
Store in an airtight container on the counter for up to 3 days or in the freezer, slices separated by parchment, for up to 3 months. Thaw at room temperature.

Tip
Make this into a traditional pound cake by omitting the lemon juice and zest. You could also then add chocolate chips and make a chocolate chip pound cake.

If you love pumpkin bread, you will definitely fall in love with this recipe. The cream cheese frosting adds just the right amount of sweetness to turn the already amazingly moist pumpkin cupcake into a scrumptious dessert. My youngest son, Rex, can smell these cupcakes being made a mile away, bringing a huge smile to his face.

Rex's Favorite Pumpkin Cupcakes

1½ cups pure cane sugar

½ cup plus 2 tbsp light vegetable oil (such as avocado oil)

2 large eggs

1 (8oz/225g) can 100% pure pumpkin

1¾ cups #1 All-Purpose Flour Blend (page 24)

½ tsp salt

1 tsp xanthan gum

1 tsp baking powder

½ tsp baking soda

½ tsp ground cinnamon

¼ tsp ground allspice

¼ tsp ground nutmeg

⅛ tsp ground cloves

⅓ cup water

Cream Cheese Frosting

½ cup salted butter, slightly softened

8oz (225g) cream cheese, firm

1 tsp pure vanilla extract

4–5 cups powdered sugar (depending on desired sweetness)

1–2 tbsp whole milk

1. Preheat the oven to 350°F (180°C) and line the muffin pans with paper liners. In the bowl of a stand mixer fitted with the whisk attachment or in a large bowl, whisk together the sugar and oil on medium speed until well combined.

2. Add the eggs and whisk on medium-high speed until well combined. Add the pumpkin and whisk on medium speed until well combined.

3. In a separate medium bowl, whisk together the #1 All-Purpose Flour Blend, salt, xanthan gum, baking powder, baking soda, cinnamon, allspice, nutmeg, and cloves.

4. Alternate adding the dry ingredients and the water into the wet ingredients, starting and ending with the flour mixture. Stir until well combined.

5. Using a ¼ cup measuring cup or ice cream scoop, fill each muffin cup about two-thirds full. Bake for 30 to 35 minutes or until a toothpick inserted into the center comes out clean. Cool completely before frosting.

Cream Cheese Frosting: In a stand mixer fitted with the paddle attachment or in a large bowl, beat the butter for 1 minute. Add the cream cheese and beat for an additional 2 minutes. Add the vanilla and powdered sugar, and beat on low speed until combined, and then increase the speed to medium and beat until fluffy, about 5 minutes. Slowly beat in the milk a few teaspoons at a time for about 1 minute, until the desired consistency is reached.

Store it

Store in an airtight container in the refrigerator for up to 5 days. Bring to room temperature before serving.

Makes:
1 (9-in/23cm) cake

Prep time:
1 hour, plus cooling
and chilling

Cook time:
40 minutes

I've always considered carrot cake to be one of the prettiest cakes, especially when you walk into a deli and the layers of cake and cream cheese frosting are staring at you from the case. The secret to this super moist cake is the pineapple, which also adds the perfect touch of sweetness.

Super Moist Pineapple Carrot Cake

1 (8oz/225g) can unsweetened crushed pineapple

4 large eggs

½ cup buttermilk

½ cup salted butter, melted

1 cup pure cane sugar

1 cup firmly packed light brown sugar

1 tsp pure vanilla extract

2 tsp apple cider vinegar

2 cups #1 All-Purpose Flour Blend (page 24)

2 tsp xanthan gum

2 tsp baking soda

2 tsp ground cinnamon

¼ tsp salt

2 cups shredded carrots

¾ cup chopped pecans, plus more to decorate

1 cup unsweetened shredded coconut

Cream Cheese Frosting (page 160)

1. Preheat the oven to 350°F (180°C). Grease and lightly flour only the bottom of two (9-in/23cm) round cake pans. Drain the pineapple, reserving 2 tablespoons of the liquid.

2. In a stand mixer fitted with the paddle attachment or in a large bowl, beat the eggs, buttermilk, butter, cane sugar, brown sugar, vanilla, and vinegar on medium-high speed until well combined.

3. In a separate medium bowl, whisk together the #1 All-Purpose Flour Blend, xanthan gum, baking soda, cinnamon, and salt.

4. Gently stir the flour mixture into the wet ingredients. Add the pineapple, 2 tablespoons reserved pineapple juice, carrots, pecans, and coconut, and stir until just combined. Let the batter sit for 5 minutes.

5. Stir the batter a couple of times and then pour equal amounts of batter into the two prepared cake pans. Bake for 35 to 40 minutes or until a toothpick inserted into the center comes out clean. Cool in the pans for 10 minutes, and then invert the cakes out of the pans onto a wire rack and cool completely.

6. Once completely cooled, frost the cake. Place one layer on a serving platter. Spread about 1 cup frosting on top of the layer, leaving about a ½-inch (1.25cm) border around the layer. Place the second layer on top and press down lightly. Use the remaining frosting to cover the top and sides of the cake. Press chopped pecans into the frosting around the cake for decoration, if desired. Refrigerate until ready to serve.

Store it

Store in an airtight container in the refrigerator for up to 5 days. Bring to room temperature before serving.

This cake is a very impressive and tasty beauty. The richness from using three different chocolates is sure to please the most avid chocolate lover. It's excellent served with strawberries or vanilla ice cream.

Glazed Triple Chocolate Bundt Cake

6oz (170g) semisweet chocolate bars

1¾ cups #1 All-Purpose Flour Blend (page 24)

1½ tsp xanthan gum

¼ cup cocoa powder

¼ tsp salt

¾ tsp baking soda

¾ tsp baking powder

¾ cup salted butter, softened

1½ cups pure cane sugar

3 large eggs

1½ tsp pure vanilla extract

2 tsp apple cider vinegar

3 tbsp chocolate syrup

¾ cup buttermilk

Glaze

½ cup heavy whipping cream

4oz (110g) semisweet chocolate bars, chopped

1. Place the oven rack in the lower third of the oven and preheat the oven to 325°F (170°C). Generously grease the entire large Bundt pan with nonstick cooking spray.

2. Melt the semisweet chocolate and set aside to cool to room temperature.

3. In a medium bowl, whisk together #1 All-Purpose Flour Blend, xanthan gum, cocoa powder, salt, baking soda, and baking powder. Set aside.

4. In a stand mixer fitted with the paddle attachment or in a large bowl, cream the butter and sugar on medium-high speed until light and fluffy, 3 to 5 minutes.

5. Beat in the eggs one at a time until incorporated. Beat in the vanilla, vinegar, chocolate syrup, and melted semisweet chocolate on medium-high speed until incorporated.

6. Reduce the speed to low and alternate adding the dry ingredients and the buttermilk into the wet ingredients, starting and ending with the flour mixture. Mix on medium speed until just combined.

7. Pour the batter into the prepared Bundt pan and bake for 60 to 75 minutes or until the cake springs back when touched and a toothpick inserted into the center comes out clean. Let cool in pan for 30 minutes and then invert onto a wire rack.

8. While the cake is still slightly warm, drizzle with the glaze, and then cool completely. Slice and serve at room temperature.

Glaze: In a small saucepan, bring the cream just to a boil over medium heat. Remove from the heat. Add the chopped semisweet chocolate to the cream. Let sit for 5 minutes, and then whisk until smooth.

Store it

Store covered in the refrigerator for up to 3 days or in individual airtight containers in the freezer for up to 3 months. Thaw at room temperature.

Tip

You can make individual Bundt cakes by using mini Bundt pans. Depending on the size of your pan, start checking for doneness after 30 minutes.

Makes:
1 (9-in/23cm) cake

Prep time:
55 minutes, plus cooling

Cook time:
30 minutes

This red velvet cake not only has a rich flavor, but also a rich, deep color and layers of cream cheese frosting. It's a beautiful cake for serving on Valentine's Day! It's one of my father-in-law's favorites, so of course I had to create a gluten-free version.

Red Velvet Cake

2½ cups #1 All-Purpose Flour Blend (page 24)

1 tsp salt

½ tsp baking soda

2 tsp baking powder

2 tsp xanthan gum

½ cup plus 3 tbsp salted butter, softened

1½ cups pure cane sugar

2 large eggs, room temperature

2 tsp pure vanilla extract

1 tbsp apple cider vinegar

3 tbsp cocoa powder

1–2 tbsp liquid red food coloring or ¾–1 tsp gel red food coloring (depending on desired color)

2–3 tbsp water

1 cup buttermilk

Cream Cheese Frosting (page 160)

1. Preheat the oven to 350°F (180°C) and line the bottoms of two (9-in/23cm) round cake pans with parchment paper. Do not grease the sides of the pans.

2. In a medium bowl, sift together the #1 All-Purpose Flour Blend, salt, baking soda, baking powder, and xanthan gum.

3. In a stand mixer fitted with the paddle attachment or in a large bowl, beat the butter on medium-high speed for 30 seconds. Beat in the sugar ¼ cup at a time, scraping down the sides of the bowl as needed after each addition. Once all of the sugar has been added, beat for an additional 2 minutes on high speed until light and fluffy.

4. Beat in the eggs one at a time until incorporated. Beat in the vanilla and vinegar.

5. In a small bowl, make a paste with the cocoa powder, food coloring, and 2 tablespoons water if using liquid food coloring or 3 tablespoons water if using gel food coloring.

6. Beat the food coloring paste into the cake batter on low speed. On low speed, alternate beating in the flour mixture and buttermilk, starting and ending with the flour mixture. Mix just until combined; do not overmix. Let sit for 5 minutes.

7. Pour the batter equally into the two prepared cake pans and bake for about 25 to 30 minutes or until a toothpick inserted into the center comes out clean and the cake bounces back when touched. Cool in the pans on a wire rack for 10 minutes. Remove the cakes from the pans and cool completely on a rack.

8. Once completely cooled, frost the cake. Place one layer on a serving platter. Spread about 1 cup frosting on top of the layer, leaving about a ½-inch (1.25cm) border around the layer. Place the second layer on top and press down lightly. Use the remaining frosting to cover the top and sides of the cake. Refrigerate until ready to serve.

Store it

Cover with plastic wrap or transfer to an airtight container and store in the refrigerator for up to 3 days.

Tip

Not everyone tolerates red food coloring, including my son and me, so we use natural food coloring in our house. Our red velvet cake is never the bright red color you see in stores or restaurants, but it still tastes and looks great. The richness and brightness in color of your cake will depend on how much food coloring you decide to use.

Makes:
1 (9-in/23cm) cake

Prep time:
45 minutes, plus cooling
and chilling

Cook time:
50 minutes

I created this recipe for my dad. He's not gluten-free, but Boston Cream Pie is his favorite dessert, and I wanted to create one that the whole family could enjoy. This cake has multiple steps and can be time consuming, but the light buttery cake, creamy vanilla custard, and rich chocolate ganache will be worth every second.

Boston Cream Pie

Pastry Cream Filling

2 cups whole milk

⅔ cup pure cane sugar, divided

6 large egg yolks

¼ cup arrowroot starch

2 tbsp salted butter

2 tsp pure vanilla extract

Cake

2½ cups #1 All-Purpose Flour Blend (page 24), plus more to flour

1 tsp xanthan gum

3 tsp baking powder

½ tsp salt

1¼ cups whole milk

⅔ cup salted butter

3 large eggs plus 1 large egg white

1½ cups pure cane sugar

2 tsp apple cider vinegar

2 tsp pure vanilla extract

Chocolate Ganache

4oz (110g) semisweet chocolate chips

½ cup heavy whipping cream

Store it

Cover and store in the refrigerator for up to 3 days.

Tip

To save time, I like to use a 5oz (140g) box of Jell-O instant vanilla pudding, prepared according to the package instructions, for the filling.

1. Prepare the pastry cream filling. While the filling is chilling, prepare the cake. Preheat the oven to 350°F (180°C). Line the bottoms of two (9-in/23cm) round cake pans with parchment paper. Do not grease the sides of the pans. In a small bowl, whisk together the #1 All-Purpose Flour Blend, xanthan gum, baking powder, and salt. Set aside. In a small saucepan, combine the milk and butter over low heat, stirring occasionally.

2. While the milk and butter are warming, in a stand mixer fitted with the paddle attachment or in a large bowl, beat the eggs, egg white, and sugar on high speed until light and fluffy, 4 to 5 minutes. Whisk in the flour mixture.

3. Increase the heat to medium-high and bring the milk and butter just to a boil, stirring constantly. Add the hot milk-butter mixture to the batter, along with the vinegar and vanilla. Whisk just until smooth.

4. Pour the batter into the prepared cake pans and bake for 22 to 25 minutes or until a toothpick inserted into the center comes out clean. Cool in the pans on a wire rack for 10 minutes. Remove the cakes from the pans and cool completely on a wire rack.

5. Once completely cooled, assemble the cake. Place one layer on a serving platter. Spread the filling on top of the layer, leaving about a ½-inch (1.25cm) border around the layer. Place the second layer on top and press down lightly. Refrigerate for 10 minutes. Pour the chocolate ganache generously over the top of the cake. Spread evenly over the top and let drip down the sides of the cake. Store in the refrigerator to firm up until ready to serve. Serve chilled or at room temperature.

Pastry Cream Filling:

1. In a medium saucepan bring the milk and ⅓ cup sugar to a boil over medium-high heat. Immediately remove from the heat. In a stand mixer fitted with the paddle attachment or in a large bowl, beat the egg yolks on medium-high speed until light and fluffy, about 1 minute. Add the arrowroot starch and remaining ⅓ cup sugar and beat on medium speed until no lumps remain.

2. Slowly whisk in ¼ cup hot milk until combined. Slowly drizzle in the remaining hot milk while constantly whisking. (If you pour all of the milk in at once, it may start to cook the eggs.) Pour the mixture back into the saucepan. Cook over medium-high heat, whisking constantly, until thickened and gently boiling. Remove from the heat and whisk in the butter and vanilla. Let cool slightly, and then cover with plastic wrap. Chill for 4 to 6 hours.

Chocolate Ganache:
Add the chocolate chips to a medium bowl. In a small saucepan, bring the cream to a boil over medium heat, stirring constantly to prevent burning. Pour the boiling cream over the chocolate chips and stir constantly until smooth. Drizzle on the cake before it thickens.

This one is for you, Jer! My brother and I LOVE funnel cakes. Occasionally on Saturday mornings when we were growing up, my dad would surprise us with homemade funnel cakes. They were SO good. So, here's my gluten-free version that's light, airy, and delicious.

County Fair Funnel Cakes

High-heat oil (such as avocado oil), for frying (2–2½ cups)

2 large eggs

2 cups whole milk

1 tsp pure vanilla extract

2 cups #1 All-Purpose Flour Blend (page 24)

1 tsp salt

2 tsp baking powder

2 tsp xanthan gum

2 tbsp pure cane sugar

4 tbsp salted butter, melted

Powdered sugar, to top

1. Line a drying rack with paper towels or newspaper. In a large frying pan, preheat 1 inch (2.5cm) of oil to 350 to 375°F (180–190°C). (This specific temperature range is important; if the oil is not hot enough, the funnel cakes will absorb too much oil and become dense and soggy.)

2. In a stand mixer fitted with paddle attachment or in a large bowl, beat the eggs on high speed until light and fluffy, about 1½ minutes. Add the milk and vanilla and beat on low speed until combined.

3. In a separate medium bowl, whisk together the #1 All-Purpose Flour Blend, salt, baking powder, xanthan gum, and sugar.

4. On low speed, beat the dry ingredients into the wet ingredients. Increase the speed to medium-high and beat until smooth, scraping down the sides as needed.

5. Fold in the melted butter with a spatula. Fill a squeeze bottle or piping bag with the batter. Creating one funnel cake at a time, squeeze the batter into the hot oil using a circular motion, overlapping the lines of batter to form a net.

6. Fry for 45 to 60 seconds until light golden brown around the edges, flip, and fry for an additional 45 to 60 seconds.

7. Carefully remove from the oil and place on the lined cooling rack to absorb the oil. Sprinkle liberally with powdered sugar and serve immediately. Repeat until you've fried all of the remaining batter.

Store it

These are best served immediately and don't reheat or store well.

Tips

This batter is thicker than a traditional gluten-filled batter and will not easily pour through a funnel like a traditional funnel cake. You will want to use a squeeze bottle or piping bag so that you can squeeze the batter into the hot oil.

If the batter does not immediately sizzle and float in the hot oil, the oil is not hot enough.

Brownies & Cookies

Mint Brownies 170

Fudgey Brownies 172

Peanut Butter Cup Brownies 173

Irresistible Pecan Squares 175

Oat Bars 176

S'mores Brownies 177

Sugar Cookies 178

Oatmeal Raisin Cookies 180

Paleo Chocolate Chip Cookies 181

Mom's Famous Chocolate
   Chip Cookies 183

Peanut Butter Cookies 184

San Luis Obispo Cowboy Cookies 185

Russian Tea Cake Cookies 186

Makes:
36 (1-in/2.5cm) squares

Prep time:
30 minutes, plus 2½ hours to cool and chill ·

Cook time:
30 minutes

These brownies remind me of a York Peppermint Pattie or Thin Mints, which I desperately miss. They combine chewy brownies with a creamy mint layer and rich chocolate ganache on top. They're outrageously delicious—I bet you can't eat just one of them.

Mint Brownies

3 large eggs

¾ cup pure cane sugar

⅔ cup firmly packed light brown sugar

½ cup salted butter, melted

1 tsp pure vanilla extract

½ cup cocoa powder

¼ cup brown rice flour

½ cup blanched almond flour

¼ cup tapioca flour

1 tsp xanthan gum

¼ tsp salt

Mint Layer

6 tbsp salted butter, softened

3 cups powdered sugar

1 tsp peppermint flavoring

6 drops green food coloring

2 tbsp whole milk, plus more if needed

Chocolate Ganache

⅔ cup semisweet chocolate chips

6 tbsp salted butter

2 tsp pure vanilla extract

1. Preheat the oven to 350°F (180°C) and lightly grease only the bottom of a 9-inch (23cm) square pan. In a stand mixer fitted with the paddle attachment or in a large bowl, beat the eggs on high speed until light and fluffy, about 2 minutes. Add the cane sugar, brown sugar, melted butter, and vanilla. Beat until well combined.

2. In a separate small bowl, whisk together the cocoa powder, brown rice flour, almond flour, tapioca flour, xanthan gum, and salt. Slowly stir the dry ingredients into the wet ingredients until well combined.

3. Pour the batter into prepared pan and bake for 25 to 30 minutes or until the center is set. Let the brownies cool completely in the pan.

4. Prepare the mint layer. In a stand mixer fitted with the paddle attachment or in a medium bowl, beat together the butter, powdered sugar, peppermint flavoring, food coloring, and milk on medium-high speed until blended. If too thick to spread, add more milk 1 teaspoon at a time until spreadable.

5. Spread the mint layer over the cooled brownies. Cover the pan with plastic wrap and refrigerate for 1 hour.

6. Prepare the chocolate ganache. In a small pan, melt the chocolate chips, butter, and vanilla over low heat, stirring frequently, until melted and smooth. Remove from the heat and allow the ganache to cool slightly, 1 to 2 minutes. Gently spread the chocolate ganache over the chilled mint layer.

7. Let the brownies set and chill in the refrigerator for at least 1 hour before cutting. Once chilled, cut the brownies into 1-inch (2.5cm) squares and serve chilled or at room temperature.

Store it

Store in an airtight container in the refrigerator for up to 1 week or in the freezer, layers separated by parchment, for up to 3 months. Thaw in the refrigerator or at room temperature.

Makes:
9 (3-in/7.5cm)
squares

Prep time:
15 minutes

Cook time:
30 minutes

Brownies are that universal dessert that just about everyone loves. This version is so rich, chewy, and delicious that no one will believe you when you tell them they are gluten-free. Serve them by themselves or as part of a brownie sundae with ice cream, chocolate syrup, whipped cream, peanuts, and a cherry on top.

Fudgey Brownies

3 large eggs

¾ cup pure cane sugar

⅔ cup firmly packed light brown sugar

½ cup salted butter, melted

1 tsp pure vanilla extract

½ cup cocoa powder

¼ cup brown rice flour

½ cup blanched almond flour

¼ cup tapioca flour

1 tsp xanthan gum

¼ tsp salt

1. Preheat the oven to 350°F (180°C) and line a 9-inch (23cm) square pan with parchment paper, leaving some hang over the sides for easy removal. In a stand mixer fitted with the paddle attachment or in a large bowl, beat the eggs on high speed until light and fluffy, about 2 minutes.

2. Add the cane sugar, brown sugar, melted butter, and vanilla. Beat on medium-high speed until well combined.

3. In a separate medium bowl, whisk together the cocoa powder, brown rice flour, almond flour, tapioca flour, xanthan gum, and salt. Slowly stir the dry ingredients into the wet ingredients until well combined.

4. Pour the batter into the prepared pan and bake for 25 to 30 minutes or until the center is set. Let cool completely in the pan. Once cooled, use the overhanging parchment paper to pull the brownies out of the pan. Cut into 3-inch (7.5cm) squares. Serve at room temperature.

Store it

Store in an airtight container on the counter for up to 3 days or in the freezer for up to 3 months. Thaw at room temperature.

Tip

To make mini brownies, thoroughly grease a mini silicone muffin pan. If you love the corner piece of brownies, this is the way to go! Once cooled, pop them out and each brownie will have that crispy, chewy edge that the corner pieces have.

Makes:
16 (2½-in/6.25cm) squares

Prep time:
15 minutes

Cook time:
35 minutes

Chocolate and peanut butter have been best friends since the beginning of time, and this recipe combines my rich and chewy chocolate brownie with sweet and salty peanut butter. It's sure to please any chocolate and peanut butter fan.

Peanut Butter Cup Brownies

3 large eggs

¾ cup pure cane sugar

⅔ cup firmly packed light brown sugar

½ cup salted butter, melted

1 tsp pure vanilla extract

½ cup cocoa powder

¼ cup brown rice flour

½ cup blanched almond flour

¼ cup tapioca flour

1 tsp xanthan gum

¼ tsp salt

1 cup chopped Reese's Peanut Butter Miniature Cups (cut into fourths), or 1 cup whole Reese's Peanut Butter Cup Minis Unwrapped (see the tip)

1. Preheat the oven to 350°F (180°C) and line a 9-inch (23cm) square pan with parchment paper, leaving some hang over the sides for easy removal. In a stand mixer fitted with the paddle attachment or in a large bowl, beat the eggs on high speed until light and fluffy, about 2 minutes.

2. Add the cane sugar, brown sugar, melted butter, and vanilla. Beat on medium-high speed until well combined.

3. In a separate medium bowl, whisk together the cocoa powder, brown rice flour, almond flour, tapioca flour, xanthan gum, and salt. Slowly stir the dry ingredients into wet ingredients until well combined.

4. Gently stir in the peanut butter cups. Pour the batter into the prepared pan and bake for 35 minutes, or until the center is set. Let cool completely in the pan. Once cooled, use the overhanging parchment paper to pull the brownies out of the pan. Cut into 2½-inch (6.25cm) squares. Serve at room temperature.

Store it

Store in an airtight container on the counter for up to 5 days or in the freezer, layers separated by parchment, for up to 3 months. Thaw at room temperature.

Tips

To avoid the hassle of unwrapping and cutting up Reese's Peanut Butter Miniature Cups (which are a smaller version of the traditional candy cup shape), I like to use Reese's Peanut Butter Cup Minis (which are even smaller candies that come unwrapped) and leave them whole. Just be careful with any seasonal shaped Reese's because they're not usually gluten-free.

If you or someone you're baking for cannot have peanut butter, this recipe is also amazing with Justin's Chocolate Almond Butter Cups.

Serves:
5 dozen (1-in/
2.5cm) squares

Prep time:
35 minutes

Cook time:
50 minutes

Pecan squares are one of my all-time favorite desserts and probably my most requested treat by family and friends. Even my husband, who very rarely eats sweets, can't resist these, especially when they're placed atop a bowl of vanilla ice cream.

Irresistible Pecan Squares

Crust
¾ cup #1 All-Purpose Flour
   Blend (page 24)
¼ cup arrowroot starch
½ cup powdered sugar
½ tsp salt
1 tsp xanthan gum
½ cup salted butter, firm and
   cut into ½-in (1.25cm) pieces

Filling
¾ cup salted butter
¾ cup firmly packed light
   brown sugar
3 tbsp honey
½ tsp pure vanilla extract
Pinch of salt
2 tbsp heavy whipping cream
3 cups chopped pecans

1. Line a 9-inch (23cm) square baking pan with parchment paper, leaving some hang over the sides for easy removal. Prepare the crust. In the bowl of a food processor fitted with the blade attachment, add the #1 All-Purpose Flour Blend, arrowroot starch, powdered sugar, salt, and xanthan gum. Pulse a few times to mix.

2. Add the butter. Pulse until pea-sized crumbs are formed. Pour the mixture into the prepared pan and press down very firmly in an even layer. Refrigerate for 15 minutes. Preheat the oven to 350°F (180°C) while the crust chills.

3. Remove the crust from the refrigerator and bake for 22 to 25 minutes or until the crust is set. Let cool while making the filling. (However, the crust does not need to be completely cooled before adding the filling.)

4. Prepare the filling. In a medium saucepan over medium-low heat, add the butter, brown sugar, honey, vanilla, and salt. Stir until the sugar is dissolved and the butter is melted.

5. Turn up the heat slightly and bring to a boil. Boil for 3 minutes, constantly stirring and scraping the sides and bottom of the pan to prevent scorching. Then remove from the heat and stir in the cream and chopped pecans. Immediately pour the pecan mixture over the crust.

6. Bake for 20 to 25 minutes or until the filling is bubbling and caramel in color. Place the pan on a rack and cool completely. Once cooled, use the overhanging parchment paper to pull the bars out of the pan. Cut into 1-inch (2.5cm) squares. Serve at room temperature.

Store it
Store in airtight container in the refrigerator for up to 5 days or in the freezer, layers separated by parchment, for up to 3 months. Thaw at room temperature or in the refrigerator.

Makes:
16 (2-in/5cm) squares

Prep time:
20 minutes

Cook time:
45 minutes

One perk of living in a small community is becoming friends with the people in town. For example, I began trading skin treatments for baked goods with my aesthetician, and she asked me to make oat bars. After a few attempts, I created this recipe, which became a fast hit. Choose between the fruit or brown sugar filling, or make a batch of both!

Oat Bars

1⅛ cups #1 All-Purpose Flour Blend (page 24)
⅓ cup firmly packed light brown sugar
⅓ cup coconut sugar
1 tsp xanthan gum
1 tsp baking powder
¼ tsp salt
1¼ cups old-fashioned rolled oats (certified gluten-free)
½ cup salted butter, firm and cut into pieces

Fruit Filling
1 (12oz/340g) jar fruit preserves (any flavor)

Brown Sugar Pecan Filling
½ cup chopped pecans
¼ cup pure cane sugar
3 tbsp #1 All-Purpose Flour Blend (page 24)
1½ tsp ground cinnamon
¼ cup salted butter, softened

1. If using the brown sugar pecan filling, prepare the filling. In a small bowl, combine the pecans, sugar, #1 All-Purpose Flour Blend, and cinnamon. Once well combined, using a pastry cutter or your hands, cut in the butter until pea-sized crumbs are formed. Set aside until ready to use.

2. Preheat the oven to 350°F (180°C) and line an 8-inch (20cm) square baking dish with parchment paper, leaving some hang over the sides for easy removal. In a large bowl, stir together #1 All-Purpose Flour Blend, brown sugar, coconut sugar, xanthan gum, baking powder, salt, and oats until well combined.

3. Using a pastry cutter or your hands, cut in the butter until evenly distributed. Press half of the mixture into the prepared pan, reserving the other half for topping.

4. Evenly spread either the fruit filling or the brown sugar pecan filling on top. Sprinkle the remaining oat mixture on top of the filling and lightly pat down.

5. Bake for 40 to 45 minutes or until light brown. Let cool completely in the pan. Once cooled, use the overhanging parchment paper to pull the bars out of the pan. Cut into 2-inch (5cm) squares. Serve at room temperature.

Store it
Store in an airtight container, layers separated by parchment, in the refrigerator for up to 3 days or in the freezer for up to 3 months. Thaw at room temperature.

One of my favorite flavor combinations is chocolate and marshmallow. You'll want to make sure you have plenty of napkins nearby, though, because these are a delicious, gooey mess. If you want, add some chopped peanuts on top of these s'mores brownies for a little bit of a salty crunch.

S'mores Brownies

3 large eggs

¾ cup pure cane sugar

⅔ cup firmly packed light brown sugar

½ cup salted butter, melted

1 tsp pure vanilla extract

½ cup cocoa powder

¼ cup brown rice flour

½ cup blanched almond flour

¼ cup tapioca flour

1 tsp xanthan gum

¼ tsp salt

3 cups miniature marshmallows

Chocolate Frosting

½ cup salted butter, melted

⅓ cup unsweetened cocoa powder

4–4½ cups powdered sugar, divided

½ cup whole milk

1. Preheat the oven to 350°F (180°C) and line a 9-inch (23cm) square deep-dish pan with parchment paper, leaving some hang over the sides for easy removal. In a stand mixer fitted with the paddle attachment or in a large bowl, beat the eggs until light and fluffy, about 2 minutes.

2. Add the cane sugar, brown sugar, melted butter, and vanilla. Beat on medium speed until well combined.

3. In a separate medium bowl, whisk together the cocoa powder, brown rice flour, almond flour, tapioca flour, xanthan gum, and salt. Slowly stir the dry ingredients into the wet ingredients until well combined.

4. Pour the batter into the prepared pan and bake for 25 to 30 minutes or until the center is set. Remove the brownies from the oven and immediately spread the marshmallows over the hot brownies. Set aside until cool.

5. Once completely cool, spread the frosting on the brownies. Use the overhanging parchment paper to pull the brownies out of the pan. Cut into 2-inch (5cm) squares. Serve at room temperature.

Chocolate Frosting: In a medium saucepan, melt the butter. Remove from the heat and stir in the cocoa powder. Stir in 2 cups powdered sugar. Add the milk and stir until smooth. Stir in enough of the remaining powdered sugar to reach a spreadable consistency.

Store it

Store in an airtight container in the refrigerator for up to 5 day or in the freezer for up to 3 months. Thaw in the refrigerator.

Makes:
about 22 (3-in/
7.5cm) cookies

Prep time:
35 minutes, plus
20 minutes to chill

Cook time:
10 minutes

These cookies are soft, buttery, and perfect on their own or decorated with icing. They've become a staple in our home during the holidays, and they work well with cookie cutters of every shape! I like to fill icing bags with different colors of icing and use a very small icing tip to decorate, or simply drizzle on the icing and add some sprinkles.

Sugar Cookies

1 cup salted butter, slightly softened

1 cup pure cane sugar

1 large egg, room temperature

1 tsp pure vanilla extract

1¾ cup white rice flour

¼ cup blanched almond flour

½ cup tapioca flour, plus more to flour

¼ cup potato starch

½ tsp baking powder

2½ tsp xanthan gum

¼ tsp salt

1. In a stand mixer fitted with the paddle attachment or in a large bowl, cream the butter and sugar on medium speed until light and fluffy, 3 to 5 minutes. Add the egg and vanilla and beat well for about 2 minutes.

2. In a separate medium bowl, whisk together the white rice flour, almond flour, tapioca flour, potato starch, baking powder, xanthan gum, and salt.

3. Slowly add the dry ingredients to the butter mixture and beat on low speed until just combined, scraping down the sides as needed; do not overmix.

4. Form the dough into two round discs and wrap in plastic wrap. Refrigerate the dough for at least 10 minutes, or up to 2 days.

5. Preheat the oven to 375°F (190°C) and line a baking sheet with parchment paper. Working in batches, on a surface lightly floured with tapioca flour, roll out one of the disks until about ¼ inch (0.5cm) thick. Keep any dough that is not being prepared in the refrigerator while waiting to be rolled, cut, and baked.

6. Using the cookie cutters of your choice, cut the dough into shapes, place on the parchment-lined baking sheet, and freeze for 10 minutes.

7. Bake one baking sheet at a time for 8 to 10 minutes. Cool on the baking sheet for 5 minutes and then transfer to a wire rack to cool completely. Repeat until all of the dough is used and decorate as desired.

Store it

Store undecorated cookies in an airtight container in the freezer. To store decorated cookies, freeze them in a single layer on a cookie sheet until hardened, and then transfer to an airtight container, layers separated by parchment. Freeze for up to 3 months. Thaw in a single layer at room temperature.

Tips

This is a great recipe to make ahead. The longer the cookie dough stays in the refrigerator (up to 2 days), the fluffier the cookies will be.

These cookies are a little fragile when freshly baked. For a sturdier cookie when decorating, make one day ahead and store in an airtight container in the freezer before decorating.

Makes:
3½ dozen

Prep time:
30 minutes, plus
30 minutes to chill

Cook time:
14 minutes

I have always loved oatmeal cookies because of the texture and all of the many different ingredients you can mix in. This recipe includes chewy and plump raisins, but you can always replace the raisins with chocolate chips, peanut butter chips, chopped Heath bar, dried cranberries, or any tiny treat.

Oatmeal Raisin Cookies

½ cup salted butter, softened

½ cup Spectrum palm shortening

⅔ cup pure cane sugar

⅔ cup firmly packed light brown sugar

2 large eggs

1 tsp pure vanilla extract

1 cup #1 All-Purpose Flour Blend (page 24)

½ cup blanched almond flour

1 tsp baking soda

1 tsp ground cinnamon

½ tsp baking powder

2 tsp xanthan gum

½ tsp salt

3 cups old-fashioned rolled oats (certified gluten-free)

1 cup raisins

1. In a stand mixer fitted with the paddle attachment or in a large bowl, beat the butter, palm shortening, cane sugar, and brown sugar on medium-high speed for 2 minutes.

2. Add the eggs and vanilla and beat on high for 3 minutes more.

3. In a separate medium bowl, whisk together the #1 All-Purpose Flour Blend, almond flour, baking soda, cinnamon, baking powder, xanthan gum, salt, and oats.

4. Add the flour mixture to the butter mixture and beat on low speed until just combined. Stir in the raisins. Cover the dough with plastic wrap and refrigerate for at least 30 minutes.

5. While the dough is chilling, place a rack in the middle of the oven and preheat the oven to 350°F (180°C). Line a baking sheet with parchment paper. Working in batches, using a 1½-inch (3.75cm) cookie scoop or a heaping tablespoon, spoon the dough onto the parchment-lined baking sheet about 2 inches (5cm) apart.

6. Bake in the middle of the oven for 12 to 14 minutes or until lightly golden brown. Cool on the pan for 2 to 3 minutes and then transfer to a wire rack to cool completely. Repeat with the remaining dough.

Store it

Store in an airtight container on the counter for up to 3 days or in the freezer for up to 3 months. Thaw in the refrigerator or at room temperature.

Tips

Make the dough and refrigerate tightly covered up to 24 hours in advance.

Have the cookie dough handy in the freezer to bake just a few at a time. You can roll the dough into a log about 2 inches (5cm) in diameter, wrap well in plastic wrap, and freeze. When ready to bake, unwrap the log and slice off ¼-inch (0.5cm) rounds. Place 2 inches (5cm) apart on the cookie sheet and bake as instructed.

If you need to use another brand of palm shortening, you may find your cookies excessively spreading. Chill the dough for at least 1 hour before baking to help prevent the spreading.

Makes:
2 dozen

Prep time:
20 minutes

Cook time:
10 minutes

There was a time when our oldest son was almost 100 percent sugar-, gluten-, and dairy-free. I created this recipe for him. They taste amazing, and you'll want to gobble them all down at once!

Paleo Chocolate Chip Cookies

⅔ cup Spectrum palm shortening

1 tbsp light vegetable oil (such as avocado oil)

¾ cup coconut sugar

¼ cup pure maple syrup

¼ cup honey

2 tsp pure vanilla extract

1½ cups blanched almond flour

½ cup arrowroot starch

¼ cup coconut flour

1 tsp salt

1 tsp xanthan gum

½ tsp baking soda

2 tsp baking powder

1½ cups dark chocolate chips

1. Place a rack in the middle of the oven and preheat the oven to 350°F (180°C). Line two baking sheets with parchment paper. In a stand mixer fitted with the paddle attachment or in a large bowl, cream together the shortening, oil, coconut sugar, maple syrup, honey, and vanilla on medium-high speed until well combined.

2. Add the almond flour, arrowroot starch, coconut flour, salt, xanthan gum, baking soda, and baking powder. Mix until well combined. Stir in the chocolate chips.

3. Let the dough sit for 10 minutes. Working in batches, using a 1½-inch (3.75cm) cookie scoop or a heaping tablespoon, spoon the dough onto the parchment-lined baking sheet about 2 inches (5cm) apart.

4. Bake one sheet at a time in the middle of the oven for 10 minutes, or until golden brown. Let cool on the baking sheet for 5 minutes, and then transfer to a wire rack to cool completely. Repeat with the remaining dough.

Store it

Store in an airtight container on the counter for up to 3 days or in the freezer for up to 3 months. Thaw at room temperature or defrost in the microwave for 30 seconds.

Tip

If you need to use another brand of palm shortening, you may find your cookies excessively spreading. Chill the dough for at least 1 hour before baking to help prevent the spreading.

Makes:
3½ dozen

Prep time:
15 minutes

Cook time:
15 minutes

I grew up eating fresh baked chocolate chip cookies from Mrs. Fields cookie shop inside our local mall, and my mom's famous cookies tasted just like a Mrs. Fields cookie—I just had to recreate the recipe. This gluten-free version is about as close as you can get to the original fresh baked cookie.

Mom's Famous Chocolate Chip Cookies

½ cup salted butter, softened

½ cup Spectrum palm shortening

1¼ cups firmly packed light brown sugar

½ cup pure cane sugar

1 tbsp pure vanilla extract

2 large eggs, room temperature

2 cups #1 All-Purpose Flour Blend (page 24)

1 cup blanched almond flour

1 tsp xanthan gum

¾ tsp salt

¾ tsp baking soda

2½ cups semi-sweet chocolate chips

1. In a stand mixer fitted with the paddle attachment or in a large bowl, cream the butter, shortening, brown sugar, and cane sugar on high speed until light and fluffy.

2. Add the vanilla and eggs and beat on medium-high speed for 3 to 4 minutes.

3. In a separate medium bowl, whisk together the #1 All-Purpose Flour, almond flour, xanthan gum, salt, and baking soda.

4. Slowly add the dry ingredients to the wet ingredients and beat on medium-low speed until combined. Gently stir in the chocolate chips. Refrigerate the dough for at least 1 hour, or up to 2 days.

5. Preheat the oven to 350°F (180°C) and line two baking sheets with parchment paper. Using a 1½-inch (3.75cm) cookie scoop or a heaping tablespoon, spoon the dough onto the parchment-lined baking sheet about 2 inches (5cm) apart. Bake one sheet at a time for 12 to 15 minutes or until the edges are light brown. Cool completely on a wire rack. Repeat with the remaining dough.

Store it

Store in an airtight container on the counter for up to 3 days or in the freezer for up to 3 months. Thaw at room temperature.

Tips

For a fluffier cookie, refrigerate the dough for at least 1 day. The fat in the dough will solidify when cold, and as the cookies bake, the solidified fat will take longer to melt. The longer the fat remains solid, the less the cookies will spread, so they come out thick and fluffy instead of flat and crunchy.

This dough freezes well. Keep the raw dough balls in an airtight container in the freezer and pop straight into the oven when ready to eat.

If you need to use another brand of palm shortening, you may find your cookies excessively spreading. Chill the dough for at least 1 hour before baking to help prevent the spreading.

Makes:
4 dozen

Prep time:
10 minutes, plus
30 minutes to chill

Cook time:
15 minutes

These peanut butter cookies are slightly crunchy on the outside and chewy on the inside with a perfect mix of sweet and salty. If you cannot have peanut butter, substitute almond butter.

Peanut Butter Cookies

1 cup salted butter, softened

1 cup peanut butter (see the tip)

2 cups firmly packed light brown sugar

2 large eggs

2½ cups #1 All-Purpose Flour Blend (page 24)

1 tsp xanthan gum

1½ tsp baking soda

1 tsp baking powder

1 cup salted peanuts (optional), chopped

Pure cane sugar, to sprinkle

1. Preheat the oven to 350°F (180°C) and line a baking sheet with parchment paper. In a stand mixer fitted with the paddle attachment or in a large bowl, beat the butter, peanut butter, and brown sugar on medium-high speed until creamy. Beat in the eggs one at a time on high speed.

2. In a separate medium bowl, whisk together the #1 All-Purpose Flour Blend, xanthan gum, baking soda, and baking powder. Stir the dry ingredients into the wet ingredients until just combined. Stir in the peanuts (if using). Refrigerate for at least 30 minutes, or up to 2 days.

3. Working in batches, using a 1½-inch (3.75cm) cookie scoop or a heaping tablespoon, spoon the dough onto the parchment-lined baking sheet about 2 inches (5cm) apart. Keep the remaining dough in the refrigerator until ready to use. Using the tines on a fork, gently press down onto the tops of the balls in a crisscross pattern. If the fork begins to stick, rinse it off and leave slightly wet. Sprinkle each cookie with cane sugar.

4. Bake one sheet at a time for 12 to 15 minutes or until a very light golden brown. Let cool on the sheet for 3 minutes and then transfer to wire rack to cool completely. Repeat with the remaining dough.

Store it

Store in an airtight container on the counter for up to 3 days or in the freezer for up to 3 months. Thaw at room temperature or defrost in the microwave for 25 seconds.

Tip

For peanut-free cookies, replace the peanut butter with almond butter and the peanuts with chopped almonds. For a nut-free version, use sunflower seed butter and sunflower seeds.

Makes:
3½ dozen

Prep time:
30 minutes, plus
1 hour to chill

Cook time:
14 minutes

San Luis Obispo is home to an incredible cookie shop downtown. When I was in college, I would buy one of their cowboy cookies every week when I went downtown to the farmers market. To this day, it's the best cookie I've ever had, so of course I created a gluten-free version. These cookies are chewy with an incredible mix of flavors.

San Luis Obispo Cowboy Cookies

1 cup Spectrum palm shortening

½ cup pure cane sugar

1½ cups firmly packed light brown sugar

2 large eggs

1 tsp pure vanilla extract

1¼ cups #1 All-Purpose Flour Blend (page 24)

1 cup blanched almond flour

1 tsp baking soda

1 tsp xanthan gum

½ tsp salt

½ tsp baking powder

½ tsp ground cinnamon

1½ cups old-fashioned rolled oats (certified gluten-free)

1 cup Heath bar pieces

1 cup mini chocolate chips

½ cup unsweetened shredded coconut

1. Place a rack in the middle of the oven and preheat the oven to 350°F (180°C). Line a baking sheet with parchment paper. In a stand mixer fitted with the paddle attachment, or in a large bowl, cream the shortening, cane sugar, and brown sugar on medium-high speed until well combined.

2. Add the eggs and vanilla and beat on medium-high speed for 4 minutes.

3. In a separate medium bowl, whisk together the #1 All-Purpose Flour Blend, almond flour, baking soda, xanthan gum, salt, baking powder, and cinnamon. Mix the dry ingredients into the wet ingredients on low speed until just combined.

4. Stir in the oats, Heath bar pieces, chocolate chips, and coconut. Cover the dough with plastic wrap and refrigerate for at least 1 hour or up to 2 days. (The longer it chills, the fluffier the cookies will be.)

5. Working in batches, using a 1½-inch (3.75cm) cookie scoop or a heaping tablespoon, spoon the dough onto the parchment-lined baking sheet about 2 inches (5cm) apart. Keep the remaining dough in the refrigerator until ready to use.

6. Bake one sheet at a time for 12 to 14 minutes or until just starting to turn golden brown. Cool on the sheet for 5 minutes and then transfer to a wire rack to cool completely. Repeat with the remaining dough.

Store it

Store in an airtight container in the freezer for up to 3 months. Thaw at room temperature or defrost in the microwave for 20 to 30 seconds.

Tips

You can bake these cookies without refrigerating the dough first. However, refrigerating for at least 1 hour will yield a bit of a fluffier and softer cookie.

If you need to use another brand of palm shortening, you may find your cookies excessively spreading. Chill the dough for at least 1 hour before baking to help prevent the spreading.

Makes:
2 dozen

Prep time:
30 minutes

Cook time:
17 minutes

My mom used to make Russian tea cakes every Christmas, and when my first gluten-free Christmas rolled around, I missed them terribly. When local shops asked me to make some special cookies for the holidays, this was the first cookie to pop into my head, and I'm so glad it was. I still look forward to these every holiday season!

Russian Tea Cake Cookies

1 cup salted butter, slightly softened

1 tsp pure vanilla extract

1 cup powdered sugar, plus 1–2 cups more to coat

2¼ cups #1 All-Purpose Flour Blend (page 24)

¼ tsp salt

1¼ tsp xanthan gum

1½ cups finely chopped walnuts or pecans

1. Preheat the oven to 350°F (180°C) and line two baking sheets with parchment paper. In a stand mixer fitted with the paddle attachment or in a large bowl, beat the butter and vanilla on high speed for 2 minutes.

2. Add the powdered sugar and beat on medium-high speed for about 5 minutes, scraping down the sides of the bowl halfway through.

3. In a separate small bowl, whisk together the #1 All-Purpose Flour Blend, salt, and xanthan gum.

4. Add the flour mixture and walnuts to the butter mixture and beat just until the dough comes together.

5. Roll the dough into 1½-inch (3.75cm) balls and place on the baking sheets 2½ inches (6.25cm) apart. The dough will be very crumbly and you will need to squeeze it together before rolling. Bake one sheet at a time for 15 to 17 minutes or until just starting to turn brown around the edges.

6. Let cool slightly on the baking sheets for 3 to 4 minutes, but do not cool all the way. Fill a small bowl with 1 to 2 cups powdered sugar. While the cookies are still warm, roll the cookies in the powdered sugar to coat completely. Set aside to cool completely on a wire rack. Once cooled, roll in the powdered sugar for a second coat, and serve.

Store it

Store in an airtight container on the counter for up to 5 days or in the freezer for up to 3 months. Thaw at room temperature. You may want to roll the cookies in more powdered sugar after they have thawed.

Tip

If your butter gets too soft or the kitchen is very hot, you can freeze or refrigerate the rolled balls of dough for 5 to 10 minutes to prevent the cookies from spreading too much.

Index

A

Afternoon Tea Blueberry Scones, 134
almond flour, 16
Almond Granola, 30
altitude, adjustments, 22
Ancient Grain Sandwich Bread, 112
Ancient Grain Waffles, 34
ancient grain flour blend, 24
apple cider vinegar, 17
Apple Crisp, 147
arrowroot flour, 16

B

Baja Fish Tacos, 50
balsamic glaze, 83
Banana Nut Bread, 122
batches, baking, 21
batters, resting, 21
BBQ Chicken Pizza, 105
beef
    Chinese Takeout Beef & Broccoli Stir-Fry, 78
    Classic Beef Stroganoff, 71
    Grandma Joy's Swiss Steak, 75
    Homemade Meatballs, 80–81
    Mama's Enchilada Pie, 76–77

    Meatloaf with Balsamic Glaze, 83
    Meaty Lasagna, 79
    Mexican Pizza, 108
    Mom's Famous Meat Sauce, 82
    Papa's Meaty Chili, 74
    Steak Sandwiches with Horseradish Cream Sauce, 72–73
Belgian Waffle Wannabes, 35
binders, 16
black beans, 50
Black Forest Cupcakes, 157
blends, flour, 18, 24
blind bake, Buttery Pie Crust, 138
Blueberry Muffins, 126–127
Boston Cream Pie, 165
Breadcrumbs, Homemade, 25
breads
    Afternoon Tea Blueberry Scones, 134
    Ancient Grain Sandwich Bread, 112
    Banana Nut Bread, 122
    Blueberry Muffins, 126–127
    Carrot Zucchini Muffins, 128
    Christmastime Cranberry Bread, 123
    Cinnamon Swirl Bread, 124
    Coffee Shop Maple Scones, 135

    Cornbread, 109
    Easy White Sandwich Bread, 113
    Flour Tortillas, 117
    Focaccia, 114–115
    Garlic Butter Naan, 110–111
    Grab 'n' Go Coffee Cake Muffins, 130
    Gruyère, Prosciutto & Chive Scones, 132–133
    Hamburger Buns, 116
    Max's Snickerdoodle Muffins, 125
    Morning Glory Muffins, 129
    Petite Vanilla Scones, 131
    Pumpkin Bread That Started It All, 120–121
breakfast
    Almond Granola, 30
    Ancient Grain Waffles, 34
    Belgian Waffle Wannabes, 35
    Chewy Granola Bars, 28–29
    Cream-Filled Donuts, 39
    Donuts 5 Ways, 40–41
    Flaky Sour Cream Biscuits, 38
    Fluffy Pancakes, 32–33
    Grandma Helen's Cinnamon Rolls, 36–37
    Traditional English Muffins, 31
brown rice flour, 16

butter, 17
buttercream frosting, 152–153
Buttery Pie Crust, 138

C

cakes
    Black Forest Cupcakes, 157
    Boston Cream Pie, 165
    Chocolate Cupcakes, 152
    Glazed Triple Chocolate Bundt Cake, 162–163
    Lemon Cupcakes with Raspberry Buttercream, 156
    Lemon Pound Cake, 158–159
    Red Velvet Cake, 164
    Rex's Favorite Pumpkin Cupcakes, 160
    Strawberry Shortcake Cupcakes, 154–155
    Super Moist Pineapple Carrot Cake, 161
    Vanilla Cupcakes, 153
California Seaside Fish 'n' Chips, 48–49
Carrot Zucchini Muffins, 128
Cheesy Rice Casserole, 93
Chewy Granola Bars, 28–29
chicken. see poultry
Chicken Parmesan, 54
Chicken Piccata, 59
Chicken Salad, 60

Chinese Takeout Beef & Broccoli Stir-Fry, 78

chocolate buttercream frosting, 152

Chocolate Cake, 152

Chocolate Cupcakes, 152

chocolate frosting, 177

chocolate ganache, 165

chocolate glaze, 40

Christmastime Cranberry Bread, 123

cinnamon glaze, 40

Cinnamon Swirl Bread, 124

Classic Beef Stroganoff, 71

cobblers, Peach Cobbler, 144–145

cocktail sauce, 47

Coffee Cake, 130

Coffee Shop Maple Scones, 135

cooling, 22

Cornbread, 109

County Fair Funnel Cakes, 166–167

Cracklin' Crab Cakes, 47

cream cheese frosting, 160

Cream-Filled Donuts, 39

Creamy White Chicken Enchiladas, 61

cross-contamination, 18

crumbly food, 22

D

dairy products, 19

dense food, 22

desserts

    Apple Crisp, 147

    Black Forest Cupcakes, 157

    Boston Cream Pie, 165

    Buttery Pie Crust, 138

    Chocolate Cupcakes, 152

    County Fair Funnel Cakes, 166–167

    Fresh Strawberry Pie, 143,

    Fudgey Brownies, 172

Glazed Triple Chocolate Bundt Cake, 162–163

Holiday Pecan Pie, 140–141

Irresistible Pecan Squares, 174–175

Lemon Cupcakes with Raspberry Buttercream, 156

Lemon Pound Cake, 158–159

Mint Brownies, 170–171

Mock Cherry Cheesecake, 146

Mom's Apple Pie, 139

Mom's Famous Chocolate Chip Cookies, 182–183

Oat Bars, 176

Oatmeal Raisin Cookies, 180

Paleo Chocolate Chip Cookies, 181

Peach Cobbler, 144–145

Peanut Butter Cookies, 184

Peanut Butter Cup Brownies, 173

Pear Tart, 148–149

Pumpkin Pie, 142

Red Velvet Cake, 164

Rex's Favorite Pumpkin Cupcakes, 160

Russian Tea Cake Cookies, 186–187

San Luis Obispo Cowboy Cookies, 185

S'mores Brownies, 177

Strawberry Shortcake Cupcakes, 154–155

Sugar Cookies, 178–179

Super Moist Pineapple Carrot Cake, 161

Vanilla Cupcakes, 153

Divine Chicken Divan, 55

Donuts 5 Ways, 40–41

doughs, resting, 21

E

Easy Crockpot Salsa Verde Pork, 67

Easy Garlic Aioli, 90–91

Easy Peasy Pizza Crust, 104

Easy White Sandwich Bread, 113

eggs, 17

entrées

    Baja Fish Tacos, 50

    BBQ Chicken Pizza, 105

    California Seaside Fish 'n' Chips, 48–49

    Chicken Parmesan, 54

    Chicken Piccata, 59

    Chicken Salad, 60

    Chinese Takeout Beef & Broccoli Stir-Fry, 78

    Classic Beef Stroganoff, 71

    Cracklin' Crab Cakes, 47

    Creamy White Chicken Enchiladas, 61

    Divine Chicken Divan, 55

    Easy Crockpot Salsa Verde Pork, 67

    Easy Peasy Pizza Crust, 104

    Grandma Joy's Swiss Steak, 75

    Heavenly Dijon Pork Chops, 66

    Homemade Meatballs, 80–81

    Linda's Luscious Pork Tenderloin, 70

    Macadamia Nut Crusted Halibut with Mango Salsa, 44–45

    Mama's Enchilada Pie, 76–77

    Meatloaf with Balsamic Glaze, 83

    Meaty Lasagna, 79

Mexican Pizza, 108

Mom's Famous Meat Sauce, 82

Oven "Fried" Chicken, 58

Papa Motte's Pork Fried Rice, 68–69

Papa's Meaty Chili, 74

Pop's Chicken Wings with Homemade Ranch Dressing, 52–53

Pork Chops with Mushroom Gravy, 64–65

Shepherd's Pie, 51

Steak Sandwiches with Horseradish Cream Sauce, 72–73

Thai Chicken Pizza, 106–107

Tuna Noodle Casserole, 46

World's Best Chicken Pot Pie, 56–57

F

fats, 19

fish. see seafood and fish

Flaky Sour Cream Biscuits, 38

Flour Tortillas, 117

flouring surfaces, 21

flours, 16

    blends, 18, 24

Fluffy Pancakes, 32–33

Focaccia, 114–115

fresh ingredients, 21

Fresh Strawberry Pie, 143

Fudgey Brownies, 172

G

Garlic Butter Naan, 110–111

Glazed Triple Chocolate Bundt Cake, 162–163

gluten, 10, 14–15

gluten-free diet, maintaining, 18

gluten-free menu items, 18

Grab 'n' Go Coffee Cake Muffins, 130

Grandma Helen's Cinnamon Rolls, 36–37

Grandma Helen's Split Pea Soup, 97

Grandma Joy's Swiss Steak, 75

greasing, 20

Gruyère, Prosciutto & Chive Scones, 132–133

gummy food, 22

H

Hamburger Buns, 116

Hawaiian Macaroni Salad, 89

Heavenly Dijon Pork Chops, 66

Holiday Pecan Pie, 140–141

Homemade Meatballs, 80–81

horseradish cream sauce, 72

I–J–K

Irresistible Pecan Squares, 174–175

kneading dough, 21

L

labels, reading, 18

leavening agents, 17

Lemon Cupcakes with Raspberry Buttercream, 156

Lemon Pound Cake, 158–159

Linda's Luscious Pork Tenderloin, 70

Loaded Baked Potato Soup, 98–99

M

Macadamia Nut Crusted Halibut with Mango Salsa, 44–45

Mama's Enchilada Pie, 76–77

mango salsa, 44

Maple Bacon Brussels Sprouts, 88

maple glaze, 40

maple icing, 135

Max's Snickerdoodle Muffins, 125

measuring, 20

Meatloaf with Balsamic Glaze, 83

Meaty Lasagna, 79

Mexican Pizza, 108

Mexican Pork Stew, 101

milk, 19

Mint Brownies, 170–171

mixing time, 20

Mock Cherry Cheesecake, 146

Mom's Apple Pie, 139

Mom's Cheesy Potatoes, 92

Mom's Famous Chocolate Chip Cookies, 182–183

Mom's Famous Meat Sauce, 82

Morning Glory Muffins, 129

muffins

    Blueberry Muffins, 126–127

    Carrot Zucchini Muffins, 128

    crowns, 22

    Grab 'n' Go Coffee Cake Muffins, 130

    Max's Snickerdoodle Muffins, 125

    Morning Glory Muffins, 129

mushiness, 22

N

number one all-purpose flour blend, 24

number two all-purpose flour blend, 24

O

Oat Bars, 176

Oatmeal Raisin Cookies, 180

oils, 19

one-to-one flour blends, 18

Oven "Fried" Chicken, 58

Oven "Fried" Zucchini, 94–95

P–Q

Paleo Chocolate Chip Cookies, 181

Papa Motte's Pork Fried Rice, 68–69

Papa's Meaty Chili, 74

pasta, store-bought, 19

pastry cream filling, 165

Peach Cobbler, 144–145

Peanut Butter Cookies, 184

Peanut Butter Cup Brownies, 173

Pear Tart, 148–149

personal care products, 18

Petite Vanilla Scones, 131

Phil's Firehouse Beans, 96

pico de gallo, 50

pies

    Buttery Pie Crust, 138

    Fresh Strawberry Pie, 143

    Holiday Pecan Pie, 140–141

    Mom's Apple Pie, 139

    Pumpkin Pie, 142

pizzas

    BBQ Chicken Pizza, 105

    Easy Peasy Pizza Crust, 104

Mexican Pizza, 108

Thai Chicken Pizza, 106–107

Pop's Chicken Wings with Homemade Ranch Dressing, 52–53

pork

    BBQ Pork Pizza, 105

    Easy Crockpot Salsa Verde Pork, 67

    Gruyère, Prosciutto & Chive Scones, 132–133

    Heavenly Dijon Pork Chops, 66

    Linda's Luscious Pork Tenderloin, 70

    Maple Bacon Brussels Sprouts, 88

    Mexican Pork Stew, 101

    Papa Motte's Pork Fried Rice, 68–69

    Pork Chops with Mushroom Gravy, 64–65

Pork Chops with Mushroom Gravy, 64–65

potato starch, 16

poultry

    BBQ Chicken Pizza, 105

    Chicken Parmesan, 54

    Chicken Piccata, 59

    Chicken Salad, 60

    Creamy White Chicken Enchiladas, 61

    Divine Chicken Divan, 55

    Mexican Pizza, 108

    Oven "Fried" Chicken, 58

    Papa's Meaty Chili, 74

    Pop's Chicken Wings with Homemade Ranch Dressing, 52–53

    Shepherd's Pie, 51

    Thai Chicken Pizza, 106–107

    World's Best Chicken Pot Pie, 56–57

powdered sugar donuts, 40

Pumpkin Bread That Started It All, 120–121

Pumpkin Pie, 142

R

ranch dressing, 52

raspberry buttercream frosting, 156

reading labels, 18

reading recipes, 22

Red Velvet Cake, 164

resting, batters and doughs, 21

Rex's Favorite Pumpkin Cupcakes, 160

Roasted Broccolini, 86–87

roasted garlic, 91

Russian Tea Cake Cookies, 186–187

S

San Luis Obispo Cowboy Cookies, 185

scones

    Afternoon Tea Blueberry Scones, 134

    Coffee Shop Maple Scones, 135

    Gruyère, Prosciutto & Chive Scones, 132–133

    Petite Vanilla Scones, 131

seafood and fish

    Baja Fish Tacos, 50

    California Seaside Fish 'n' Chips, 48–49

    Cracklin' Crab Cakes, 47

    Macadamia Nut Crusted Halibut with Mango Salsa, 44–45

    Tuna Noodle Casserole, 46

Shepherd's Pie, 51

sides

    Cheesy Rice Casserole, 93

    Cornbread, 109

Grandma Helen's Split Pea Soup, 97

Hawaiian Macaroni Salad, 89

Loaded Baked Potato Soup, 98–99

Maple Bacon Brussels Sprouts, 88

Mom's Cheesy Potatoes, 92

Oven "Fried" Zucchini, 94–95

Phil's Firehouse Beans, 96

Roasted Broccolini, 86–87

Smashed Sweet Potatoes with Easy Garlic Aioli, 90–91

Smashed Sweet Potatoes with Easy Garlic Aioli, 90–91

S'mores Brownies, 177

snacks, 18

sorghum flour, 16

soups and stews

    Mexican Pork Stew, 101

    Papa's Meaty Chili, 74

    Taco Soup, 100

spreading, 22

Steak Sandwiches with Horseradish Cream Sauce, 72–73

stews. *see* soups and stews

storage, foods, 22

Strawberry Shortcake Cupcakes, 154–155

Sugar Cookies, 178–179

sugars, 17

Super Moist Pineapple Carrot Cake, 161

sweet loaves

    Banana Nut Bread, 122

    Christmastime Cranberry Bread, 123

    Cinnamon Swirl Bread, 124

    Coffee Cake, 130

    Pumpkin Bread That Started It All, 120–121

T–U–V

taco seasoning, 100

Taco Soup, 100

tapioca flour, 16

tartar sauce, 49

teff flour, 16

temperature of ingredients, 21

Thai Chicken Pizza, 106–107

Traditional English Muffins, 31

Tuna Noodle Casserole, 46

Vanilla Cupcakes, 153

vanilla glaze, 40

W–X–Y–Z

wheat, 10

whipped cream, 35, 143

whipped cream frosting, 157

white rice flour, 16

white sauce, 50

World's Best Chicken Pot Pie, 56–57

xanthan gum, 16

About the Author

Jennifer Fisher is a gluten-free recipe developer. When she went gluten-free in 2009, she was determined to make all the food she still loved. So, she dedicated her time to experimenting endlessly in the kitchen, which turned into a small baking business where she sold gluten-free baked goods to a few local stores—gluten-free labels aside, customers would never know her scrumptious treats were gluten-free! It quickly became a raving success, and she received order requests from local health food markets and coffee shops, as well as requests to bake for private parties and gatherings. She ultimately shuttered her business to focus on her family, but her community never stopped asking about her delicious treats. Jennifer wrote them all down in her first cookbook, *Surprise! It's Gluten-Free!* She lives in San Clemente, a small beach town in Southern California, with her husband Kirk, their two sons Max and Rex, and their dog Fletch.

Acknowledgments

This book has been a group effort and would never have been published without the encouragement, love, and support from so many people. Writing a book and caring for two boys is not an easy task, but my in-laws and parents helped me to get it all done. Thank you C.P., Linda, Mom, and Dad for your countless hours of driving our boys to wherever they needed to go when I would call in a panic because I had loaves of bread in the oven, for washing mountains of dishes, for baking with me in the kitchen, and most of all for eating all of my creations!

When I set out to write my first cookbook, I was extremely overwhelmed. I knew how to develop recipes and write them down, but I had no idea how to transform my recipes into a manuscript worthy of sending to a publisher. Mikal Belicove, you worked miracles and turned my recipes written down on scratch pieces of paper into an actual manuscript! Thank you for believing in me, for taking on this project, and for convincing others that I'm worth investing in. This book would definitely not be in existence without you. Thank you friend!

Alexandra Andrzejewski, my editor, has been a complete joy to work with! Thank you for guiding me, encouraging me, teaching me, and most of all for your kindness and patience. This book would never be what it is without you! Thank you also to the creative team who brought my recipes to life, including Rebecca Batchelor, Lovoni Walker, Ashley Brooks, and Kelley Schulyer.

My mom is a special lady to whom I owe an endless amount of thanks. Not only did she teach me how to cook from a very young age, but she was also the inspiration and original author of so many recipes in this book. Thank you for the hours and hours you spent in the kitchen with me cooking and baking so I could meet my deadlines. You are always there when I need you. Dad, thank you for the many hours you spent entertaining the boys so I could cook and meet deadlines. And thank you for being willing to test every recipe I ever created!

Everything I do, I do for my boys. Thank you Max and Rex for being the most patient and loving two boys for whom a mom could ever ask. You are my biggest inspirations and I love you both more than you could ever imagine. Max, you have believed in me from day 1 and have always been my number one fan. You are the best taste tester I could ever have. I will never stop creating recipes for you!

This book would not be in existence without my husband. He always believed in me even when I didn't believe in myself. My number one job is to be a wife and mother, but with his encouragement and endless hours of washing dishes and staying up late to take the last batch of cookies out of the oven, I have been able to pursue my passion for helping others with restricted diets. Thank you for being my everything and for all of the selfless acts you do for the boys and me. You are my number one, and I love you.